ORGANIZATIONAL CLIMATE IN CO-OPERATIVE SECTOR -

JULY 1991

CONTENTS

ACKNOWLEDGEMENTS

I record my sincere gratitude and obligation to Dr. A. VENKATACHALAM, M.Com., M.Phil., M.B.A., Ph.D., Lecturer - Selection Grade, Department of Commerce, N.M.S.S. Vellaichamy Nadar College, Nagamalai, Madurai-19 under whose able guidance the dissertation was completed. He was deeply involved in the dissertation right from the formulation of the problem till its completion.

I am profusely greatful to Dr. K. NATARAJAN, M.Com., M.Phil., Ph.D., Professor and Head, Department of Commerce, N.M.S.S. Vellaichamy Nadar College, Madurai-19 for his invaluable encouragement till the completion of the study.

I wish to record my sincere thanks to the officials and employees of co-operative spinning mills, for their willing co-operation and help to complete this study.

My thanks are due to Mr. T. VANNIARAJAN, M.A., M.Phil., M.B.A., Lecturer, Department of Business Administration, N.M.S.S. Vellaichamy Nadar College, for his help in processing the data.

I express my heartful thanks to Mr. K. RAMASAMY who has gone through the draft dissertation and offered suggestions.

I thank my friend Mr. Ponpandian, M.Com.,PGDBA.,
PGDCA, (Pragati Computers) for his support in all possible
ways in completing this work.

I shall be failing in my duty if I do not express
my gratitude to my parents and my brothers Mr. Srither,B.Sc.,
Mr. Rajaram, M.A., without whose collective encouragements
and good wishes the successful completion of this study
would not have been possible.

Finally I thank Mr. Murali who has made the presen-
tation attractive by efficient typing.

                         S. SENBAGANATHAN.

LIST OF TABLES

viii

TABLE NO   PAGE

CHAPTER I

INTRODUCTION

The term Organizational Climate is defined as a
relatively enduring quality of the internal environment
of an organization as perceived and experienced by members,
which can be described in terms of specific dimensions or
characteristics and which influences the patterns of behaviour and work performance of others. It is the totality
of interesting and inter-related internal characteristics
which significantly influence the motivation of members.
Organizational Climate evolves over a fairly long period of
time and is relatively stable. Due to the rapid changes in
the pursuit of technological changes, the employers have
neglected the personnel of the organization, resulting in
the low morale of the workers and many trade conflicts and
disputes. To avoid such untoward incidents, at present,
every organization is attempting to create a favourable
atmosphere within the organization, which will ensure better
performance and efficiency of the workers. When one speaks
of a favourable atmosphere one should be aware of the various
things that the employees expect from their job. To understand the wants of the employees, the management should have
an awareness of the perceptions of the members of the system,
of the various characteristics of the organization. By

bringing their sensitivity closer and closer to employee's perceptions, they can often increase their effectiveness in working with employees. The perception of the employees of the various characteristics of an organization is known as the 'Climate' of the organization.

One cannot see the climate or touch it, but it is there. Like the air in a room, it surrounds and affects everything that happens in an organization. In turn, climate is affected by almost everything that occurs in an organization. Organizations like, finger prints and snow flakes, are always unique. Each has its own culture, traditions and methods of action which in their totality, constitute its climate. Some organizations are bustling and efficient; others are easy going. Some are quite human; others are hard and cold. An organization tends to attract and keep people who fit into its climate, so that its patterns are to some extent perpetuated. Just as people may choose to move to a certain geographic climate of sea, mountains or desert, they also will choose the Organizational Climate they prefer.

Climate can influence motivation, performance and job satisfaction. It does this by creating certain kinds of

1. Keith Davis, Human Behaviour at Work, Tata McGraw Hill Book Company, New Delhi, 1985, p.104.

expectations about the nature of consequences that will follow from different actions. Employees expect certain rewards, satisfactions and frustrations on the basis of their perception of the organization's climate. These expectations tends to load to motivation. A sound climate is a long run proposition. Managers need to take an assets approach to climate, meaning that they take the long run view of climate as an organizational asset. Unwise discipline and putting pressures on people may temporarily get better performance, but at the cost of the asset called climate.[2]

Organizational Climate is a system and holistic concept; the interacting effect among the elements creating the climate which is more than the sum of the effects of individual elements. An employee perceives the texture of different elements of the Organizational Climate in his own way depending upon his previous experience, state of learning and understanding so on, Organizational Climate reflects also the history, of internal and external struggles, the types of people the Organization attracts, its work processes and physical layout, the modes of communication, and the exercise of authority within the system.[3]

2. Ibid.

3. Daniel Kalz, Robert. L. Kahn, The Social Psychology of Organizations, Wiley Easter Private Limited, New Delhi, 1970, p.66.

Organizational Climate is closely related with productivity. Productivity depends upon the nature of the work, involvement in the work satisfaction in the job, physical environment, work group and relationship with the supervisors. All these factors are the integral part of Organizational Climate. To make an organization successful it should have a conducive climate to work.

Perception of the worker, about the organization differs from one to another. It differs from one age group to another age group, mill to mill, department to department and so on. No two persons are similar in mental abilities, traditions, sentiments and behaviours; they differ widely also as groups and are subject to many and varied influences.[4] This study is an attempt to measure the attitude of workers and employees of co-operative spinning mills in Madurai district towards their Organizational Climate.

1.2   STATEMENT OF THE PROBLEM

Individuals as human beings are very complex in their psychological make-up. When they interact with one

---

4.   Memoria, C.B., _Personnel Management_, Himalaya Publishing House, Bombay, 1984, p.3.

another in groups and especially in large organizations, complexities are multiplied, To understand an individual, it becomes eventually necessary to study what a person is and what he does. The former represents the personality and the latter represents the behaviour. The environment or climate (stimulus) has vital role to play in shaping the personality as well as the behaviour. The function of the personality and environment may produce different behaviours and some behaviour may be exerted under different stimulus situations. Keeping this in view, in organization system, the behaviour of the organizational participants is largely determined by the climate of the organization. The organizations, in order to get maximum results from the individuals, try to provide a climate which may facilitate achieving of such results.

The better functioning of the organization depends upon the satisfaction of the workers. Mostly the amount of satisfaction they enjoy may depend on their attitude towards the Organizational Climate. The factors influencing the climate are working condition job characteristics, workers attitude, performance-reward relationship, personal policies, communication and supervision. Rapid industrial development and attainment of economic self-reliance are the two major

tasks of our country. It is achieved by increased productivity and enchanced production which depends upon the efficienc
and effort of the workers. Productivity can be increased
only when there is co-operation between labour and management.
Each worker in an organization has to do his best for the
development of himself and organization to which he belongs.
The way to ensure this is to create such a climate in an
organization, where the workers have to satisfy their social
and psychological needs besides their economic needs. Good
climate reduces absentism, strike and labour turnover in an
organization.

Textile industry is one of the traditional industries
in India. It provides direct employment to nearly 20% of
the nation's industrial labour. Moreover, it accounts for
1/5 of the country's industrial production. The industry has
three sub-sectors namely mill sector, powerloom sector and
handloom sector. There are nearly 875(1984) textile mills
in the country out of which 65% are spinning mills and the
rest are weaving mills.[5] Strikes, lock outs and other
industrial problems are common features of concerns industry

---

5. Subramanian, N., Workers Attitude towards Organizational
   Climate, - A Study on Textile Mill in Madurai, (An unpubli
   shed dissertation, M.K. University), 1986.

problems are causing great concern not only to the employers, administrators, but also to the workers themselves.

In TamilNadu, next to Coimbatore Madurai district has heavy concentration of textile units. Just like other textile units in other parts of the country, in Madurai district also textile units are suffering a lot from the view point of the employers as well as the workers. How far the Organizational Climate in textile units is conducive for maintaining a good relationship between the employers and workers. In the present study, the researcher has made an attempt to study the existing Organizational Climate, and attitude towards the Organizational Climate in co-operative spinning mills of Madurai district in all levels of employment.

1.3   REVIEW OF PREVIOUS STUDIES

A review of the previous studies on Organizational Climate is essential to understand the intricacies of the problems selected for the study and also to know the areas already investigated, so that the new areas hitherto unexplored may be studied indepth.

Litwin and stringer have included six factors which affect Organizational Climate. These are

i) organization structure-perceptions to the extent of organizational constraints, rules, regulations red-tape;(ii)individual responsibility-feelings of the autonomy of being one's own boss (iii) rewards-feelings related to being confident of adequate and appropriate rewards (iv) risk and risk taking perceptions of the degree of challenge and risk in the work situation (v) warmth and support-feelings of general good fellowship and helpfulness prevailing in the work settings; and (vi) tolerance and conflict-degree of confidence that the climate can tolerate differing opinions.[6]

A broad and somewhat more systematic study of climate dimensions described by Schneider and Barlett includes six items that should be included in determining Organizational Climate.   These are managerial support, managerial structure, concern for new employees, inter-agency conflict, agent dependence and general satisfaction.[7]

Taguiri has identified five factors in Organizational Climate on the basis of the information provided by managers.

---

6. Litwin G.H. and Stringer, R., The Influence of OC on Human Motivation, Quoted in Prasad, L.M., Organization Theory an Behaviour, Sultan Chand & Sons, New Delhi, 1984, p.377.
7. Schneider and Barlott, Individual Differences and OC, Quoted in L.M. Prasad, Idem.

These are (i) practices relating to providing a sense of
direction or purpose to their jobs-setting of objectives,
planning and feed back; (ii) opportunities for exercising
individual initiative; (iii) working with a superior who
is highly competitive and competent. (iv) working with
co-operative and pleasant people: and (v) being with a
profit minded and sales oriented company. Taiguri and
Litwin (1968) define Organizational Climate as a relatively
enduring quality of the internal environment that is experienced by its members that influences their behaviours and
that can be described in terms of the values of a particular
set of characteristics of the organization. Fried Lander
and Margulies (1969) also define organizational climate as a
relatively stable or on going property of the organization
which may release, channel, facilitate constrain on an organization's technical as well as human resources.[8]

Pritchard and Karasick (1973) define Organizational
Climate as a relatively enduring quality of the internal
environment of an organization distinguishing it from other

---

8. Friedlander, R., Margulis, N. Effects of Job Attitudes
     Training and OC, Journal of Applied Psychology, 1971,
     Vol.55, pp.287-295.

organizations which (a) results from the behaviour and polici
of the top management (b) is preceived by the members, (c)
serves as a basis for interpreting the situation, and (d) act
as a source of pressure for directing activity.[9]

Dr. A.K. Srivastava in his study "Motivation and
perception of Organizational Climate" has made an attempt
to examine the effect of employees' achievement on their
perception of Organizational Climate. In his study he has
taken the factors like nature of work, responsibility rewards
risk standards of performance and identity with organization
as components of Organizational Climate. The results of the
investigation indicate that, the employees motivated with
differentical strength by achievement. Significantly differ
from each other with regard to their perception of most of
the dimensions of Organizational Climate.

K.B. Akhilesh and S.Pandey in their study, "A comparative study of Organizational Climate in two banks" have

---

9. Pritchard, R.P. and Karasick, B.W., The Effects of OC
   on Managerial Job Performance and Job Satisfaction,
   Organizational Behaviour and Human Performance Review,
   1973, pp.126-149.

pointed out that nationalised bank has better attitudinal
profile over private sector bank. In their opinion. There
is better recognition and rewards for performance in private
sector banks. It appears that this relationship is the
strengthened area of the private sector bank over nationalised
bank. The study further revealed that the private sector
has a slighted task oriented climate.[10]

Gupta stresses the importance of human element in
industry which is an indispensable factor for achieving the
objectives of any industry and the factor includes both
physical and physiological aspects of work. Out of human
factors, the author says that worker's attitude and morale
are of utmost importance. He also feels that, to motivate
a person, the first thing to be noted is that whether right
man is on the right job only then he feels that job satisfaction could be attained. Moreover factors like proper
training and information, wage incentives and bonus,optimum
working environment, delegation of responsibility, opportunities of promotion, introduction of non-monetary benefits
are to be given due importance to motivate and to induce high

10. Akhilesh, K.B. & Pandey, S., A Comparative Study of
    Organizational Climate in Two Banks, IJIR, Vol.XXI,
    No.4, April 1986, pp.458-459.

morale in a worker. He finally concludes by saying that these are not the only means to motivate the people. Motivational requirements differ from person to person and that the manager must be intelligent enough to appraise these needs and tailor his approach to suit both the needs of the people and of the situation.[11]

1.4   SCOPE OF THE STUDY

In India the performance of co-operative spinning mill is not satisfactory when compared with that of the private spinning mills. Instead of talking about various issues related to poor performance of co-operative spinning mills, it is worthwhile to findout how we can improve the performance of co-operative spinning mills.

The changing concepts about the management of industrial organizations require a new look at the concept of performance as well. In the past, performance was defined in terms of a rise in the level of output of services with the same or reduced level of input as a result of better

---

11. Gupta, M.C., "Mechanism of Motivation and Morale in Industry", Personnel Today, Jan-March, 1986.

work methods and improved technology. It is, however,through
the employees that the ultimate increase in production is
achieved. Their performance is more important than equipment
and raw materials. If they are not motivated to work harder
and better, with sincerity, initiative and co-operation, no
amount of sophisticated technology or improved work method is
going to help. Therefore, performance need to be redefined
in terms of employee's motivation and satisfaction. Every
employee's satisfactory performance is vital to the proper
functioning of machinery and equipment in the industry, and
productivity is more likely to be determined by what the
employees do rather than what the machines can do (A. Sharma,
1987).

Managing the employees today is an increasingly
difficult task. The involvement, sincerity, creativity and
dedication to the job that the management expects do not seem
to be the outcome of financial incentives as it was believed
earlier. It is observed that inspite of adequate incentives,
motivation to better performance is still lacking. Performance
can be improved in two ways. Good employees who could perform
the task in a dependable manner and also use their creativity
in their job performance can be attracted. On the other hand,

the organisation should give them a working culture, a climate that enhances their growth and fulfils their expectations.

It has been empirically proved in many Indian and western organisations that conducive work climate, employee-centred climate and achievement-oriented climate ultimately improve performance (Litwin & Stringer, 1968) Cawsey, 1973, Likert, 1961). It was decided to undertake the study in Silk mill and good working mill within a district. So, Madurai district was selected for this study. In Madurai district there are three co-operative spinning mills. Madurai District Co-operative Spinning Mill-Melur, Anna Co-operative Spinning Mill-Andipatti and another one in Koothiyargundu. Melur mill is the sick mill and the other two are working well. It is decided to measure the Organizational Climate in one sick mill and good working mill. So, this study confines to Madurai District Co-operative Spinning Mill and Anna Co-operative Spinning Mill.

1.5   OBJECTIVES OF THE STUDY

The present study on "Organizational Climate in co-operative sector-A Study on co-operative spinning Mills" has been conducted with the following specific objectives.

(i)   To highlight the existing Organizational Climate
       prevailing in co-operative spinning mills.

(ii)   To study the perception and attitude of the employees
       towards various factors affecting the Organizational
       Climate.

(iii) To find out the extent of relationship between socio-
       demographic factors and Organizational Climate.

(iv)   To make suitable suggestions on the basis of the
       study.

1.6   HYPOTHESES

       The following hypotheses were framed for testing
the factors influencing the Organizational Climate in co-operative spinning mills in Madurai District.

       i)   Age of the employees has association with
            Organizational Climate.

       ii) Educational qualification of the employees has
            association with organizational climate.

iii) Level of management has influence over organizational climate.

iv) Work experience of the employee has association
with organizational climate.

v) Income of the employee influences the attitude
of employees towards organizational climate.

vi) Social group of the employee influences the
attitude of employees towards organizational
climate.

1.7   METHODOLOGY AND TOOL

The present study is based on survey method. It
involves survey of employees in different level management
of co-operative spinning mills in Madurai district. The
data relating to organizational climate has been collected
directly from employees of selected units through personal
interview.   An interview schedule has been used as an
instrument for collecting the data (Vide Appendix-I).
Although it was not a standardized questionnaire previously
used by researchers, the climate dimensions incorporated in

this interview schedule were based on the determinants of
climate identified by some of the earlier researchers. This
interview schedule contains 49 statements grouped under the
following seven dimensions.

i) Worker's Attitude :

Towards peers, the management and others; a sense
of belongingness to the organization.

ii) Job Characteristics :

Provisions of realistic job design, job preview
job pressures etc., sense of freedom felt in the job.

iii) Working Conditions :

Provisions of safe and healthy working conditions;
adequate job security; realistic and reasonable work standards,
and adequate welfare facilities and amenities to employees
and their families at their work place and outside.

iv) Personnel Policies :

Selection, criteria based on ability; degree to
which promotions are based on performance; adequate facilities

for general education and technical training; existence of
a sound grievance-handling procedure; attractive retirement
benefits.

v) Performance-Reward Relationship :

Individualised reward system; degree to which
rewards are fair and appropriate.

vi) Supervision :

Supervisors ability in finding out mistakes,
encouragement by the supervisors, supervisor-sub ordinate
relationship, supervisory capacity.

vii) Communication :

Communication gap, informal communication, friendly
advise, formal communication and informal interaction among
workers, workers and employers.

Each respondent was asked to respond to the 49
statements using the Likert type 5 point scoring system,
ranging from strongly agree (5) to strongly disagree(1).

The analysis, findings and conclusions of this study are mostly based on the information generated by interview schedule. Hence it is necessary to be sure wehther the information thus generated is indeed reliable. An attempt was therefore made to test the reliability of the instrument in terms of its two major characteristics.

(a) The analysis was based on aggregate data Individual's aggregate scores were obtained by pooling the responses of each respoi.dent to the seven dimensions. Hence, it is necessary to verify the inter-item consistency of responses among the seven dimensions for the sample as a whole.

(b) In this study, climate is assumed to be a multidimensional concept. Seven different dimensions are used to measure each dimension. It is thus important to verify whether the seven statements used to measure each dimension belong to that dimension rather than any other.

TABLE : 1.1 INTER CORRELATION MATRIX FOR EACH OF THE SEVEN DIMENSION OF ORGANIZATIONAL CLIMATE

SER. NO:	ONE	TWO	THREE	FOUR	FIVE	SIX	SEVEN
1	1.0000						
2	0.5065	1.00000					
3	0.6329	0.4821	1.00000				
4	0.4596	0.4433	0.5631	1.0000			
5	0.4905	0.5231	0.4729	0.5253	1.0000		
6	0.5458	0.5761	0.5211	0.4284	0.4321	1.00000	
7	0.4905	0.3935	0.3656	0.4729	0.4102	0.5323	1.0000

* All Correlation Co-efficients reported above are positive and satisfactory significant at .01 level.

TABLE 1.2   ITEM TO TOTAL CORRELATION CO-EFFICIENTS   BETWEEN EACH 21 ITEM SCORE AND SCORE FOR EACH OF 7 DIMENSIONS OF ORGANIZATIONAL CLIMATE

:	ONE	TWO	THREE	FOUR	FIVE	SIX	SEVEN
1	0.64	0.58	0.43	0.27	0.20	0.23	0.39
2	0.58	0.38	0.39	0.51	0.46	0.47	0.30
3	0.54	0.22	0.31	0.24	0.43	0.49	0.27
4	0.61	0.52	0.08	0.27	0.23	0.11	0.19
5	0.49	0.43	0.39	0.21	0.41	0.16	0.23
6	0.48	0.37	0.36	0.27	0.29	0.10	0.09
7	0.65	0.49	0.42	0.36	0.23	0.05	0.51
8	0.41	0.69	0.39	0.46	0.52	0.23	0.30
9	0.48	0.57	0.11	0.19	0.09	0.36	0.39
10	0.32	0.60	0.26	0.25	0.33	0.24	0.47
11	0.09	0.57	0.29	0.32	0.46	0.09	0.16
12	0.30	0.55	0.28	0.34	0.13	0.12	0.27
13	0.36	0.61	0.25	0.46	0.29	0.14	0.53
14	0.38	0.66	0.52	0.49	0.27	0.29	0.55
15	0.36	0.34	0.70	0.59	0.61	0.38	0.34
16	0.07	0.23	0.43	0.34	0.28	0.29	0.05
17	0.38	0.27	0.54	0.23	0.17	0.32	0.14
18	0.42	0.26	0.61	0.27	0.23	0.43	0.46
19	0.23	0.39	0.62	0.29	0.18	0.29	0.28
20	0.34	0.43	0.55	0.42	0.34	0.36	0.09
21	0.20	0.41	0.49	0.34	0.32	0.33	0.19
22	0.22	0.33	0.17	0.41	0.34	0.26	0.18
23	0.25	0.16	0.36	0.48	0.11	0.24	0.12
24	0.34	0.24	0.29	0.72	0.34	0.36	0.34
25	0.36	0.18	0.26	0.54	0.28	0.25	0.13
26	0.29	0.23	0.44	0.63	0.18	0.34	0.29
27	0.19	0.53	0.51	0.62	0.23	0.39	0.34
28	0.24	0.11	0.25	0.61	0.29	0.41	0.40
29	0.36	0.29	0.28	0.13	0.48	0.29	0.26
30	0.42	0.40	0.34	0.27	0.64	0.28	0.43
31	0.46	0.37	0.28	0.43	0.73	0.61	0.29
32	0.51	0.46	0.29	0.29	0.67	0.57	0.58
33	0.29	0.09	0.28	0.13	0.58	0.43	0.39
34	0.27	0.29	0.43	0.41	0.59	0.44	0.41
35	0.34	0.18	0.27	0.29	0.50	0.31	0.24
36	0.26	0.41	0.43	0.38	0.32	0.47	0.31
37	0.24	0.34	0.27	0.39	0.42	0.44	0.29
38	0.34	0.18	0.29	0.47	0.44	0.53	0.34
39	0.38	0.33	0.29	0.42	0.53	0.54	0.26
40	0.52	0.15	0.43	0.29	0.23	0.63	0.43
41	0.18	0.27	0.49	0.27	0.47	0.62	0.54
42	0.23	0.49	0.54	0.57	0.39	0.61	0.50
43	0.54	0.23	0.34	0.42	0.46	0.40	0.58
44	0.29	0.34	0.59	0.63	0.68	0.34	0.73
45	0.26	0.38	0.29	0.47	0.52	0.51	0.54
46	0.39	0.37	0.34	0.36	0.44	0.40	0.46
47	0.41	0.43	0.29	0.27	0.23	0.46	0.48
48	0.29	0.44	0.26	0.45	0.32	0.43	0.50
49	0.37	0.30	0.24	0.09	0.29	0.04	0.39

* Figure shown inside Diagonal boxes represent Correlation of each item score with the total score of the Dimension in which the item has been included

Table 1.1 gives the inter-item correlations among
the seven dimensions of organizational climate. All correlations presented in the table are positive and statistically
significant, and it suggests that there is reasonable inter-
item agreement among individual's scores for the seven dimensions of organizational climate for the sample as a whole.
Hence, aggregating the responses of each respondent across
the dimensions is justified.

That each of the 49 statements belongs to the
climate dimension in which it is intended to be included can
be seen from the item-to-total correlations presented in
Table 1.2. There are 343 correlations presented in this
table, of which 49 have been singled out and placed within
diagonal boxes. Since each item is intended to measure a
part of one of the dimensions of Organizational Climate.
The total score represents a more complete measure of each
dimension. It follows from this that each item score should
correlate positively with the total score of the dimension
in which it is included. If an item really belongs to the
dimension in which it has been included, then its correlations
shown inside the box should be higher than any of its correlations outside the box. A close examination of Table 1.2
shows that this condition is met for each of the 49 items.

This shows that responses to statements pertaining to the ten
dimensions of Organizational Climate are internally consistent
and reliable. It also indicates that the seven statements
used to measure each dimension belong only to that dimension
rather than to any other.

It can therefore be said that (i) there is adequate
agreement among the responses to the set of statements under
each of the ten dimensions designed to measure a given respondent's climate total score; and (ii) each statement truly
belongs to the dimension of Organizational Climate in which
it has been included.

The same interview schedule was administered to the
subjects of all levels of management. The scores obtained
were classified into three groups of climate raters.

Organizational Climate	Score	
	Melur	Andipatti
Rated as GOOD	175 to 245	165 to 245
Rated as MODERATE	128 to 174	121 to 164
Rated as NOT GOOD	Less than 128	Less than 121

1.8   SAMPLING DESIGN

The total population is 1322; Madurai district
Co-operative Spinning Mill 877.   Anna Co-operative Spinning
Mill 445.   Samples were selected randomly after stratifying
into top management (3+3), middle management(72+32) and lower
management (802+408).   In top management purposive sampling
(2+2) has been adopted.   In middle management 25% of the
employees in each mill, (18+9) and 10% of the workers (81+41)
in each mill have been selected randomly.   Table 1.3 explains
about sample selection.

TABLE 1.3

Sample Selection

Level of Management	MELUR		ANDIPATTI	
	Total	Sample	Total	Samp
Top Management	3	2	3	
Middle Management	72	18	32	
Lower Management	802	81	408	4
Total	877	101	443	5

Grand Total (Population)   =   1320

Sample   =   153

Nearly 12% of the Population.

1.9   DATA COLLECTION AND ANALYSIS

The primary data were collected by the researcher
himself.   The field work was conducted for a period 3 months
i.e. from January 1991 to March 1991.

In this study, the data were analysed by using
statistical method like correlation, mean, standard deviation and chi-square test.   Attitude of the employees towards
Organizational Climate has been measured through likert scale.
A scoring scheme has been evolved to quantify the data.

1.10   CHAPTER SCHEME

This first chapter deals with the design of the
study.   It begins with introduction and includes review of
previous study, statement of the problem, scope of the study,
objectives, hypotheses, methodology and tool, sampling design,
collection of data, statistical analysis and scheme of report.

The second chapter "Organizational Climate - An Overall Theoritical View" explains Organizational Climate and its importance.

The third chapter "Employees Attitude towards Organizational Climate - Pertaining to Personal Factors" explains the employees attitude towards Organizational Climate on the basis of their age, educational qualification and social group.

The fourth chapter "Employees Attitude towards Organizational Climate - Pertaining to Job Factors" explains the employees attitude towards Organizational Climate on the basis of their, level of management, work experience and Income

The fifth chapter "Organizational Climate - An Informal Appraisal" explains about the views and attitudes of employees towards their Organizational Climate. This chapter mainly presented with the help of informal interview, interaction with employees when they were free to know about their actual feelings regarding their Organizational Climate. It helps to find out the difference between attitude expresse by the employees through interview schedule.

The sixth chapter "Summary and Conclusion" summarise the entire study and makes a report of the findings. Based on this a few suggestions are also given to improve the Organizational Climate.

CHAPTER II

ORGANIZATIONAL CLIMATE - AN OVERALL THEORITICAL VIEW

2.1   INTRODUCTION

The term "Organization" is a word that can be
used in a number of ways.   We can speak of organization
as the activity that is an important function of management.   In the words of Mooney and Reiley Organization is
the form of every human association for the attainment of
a common purpose.[1]   In other words organization is simply
people working together for a common goal.

All organizational theoreticians and researchers
unanimously agree that a sound climate is extremely important
for the ultimate achievement of organizational goals.
Organizational Climate though abstract in concept is normally
associated with job performance and job satisfaction and
morale of the employees.   Climate is a commonly experienced
phenomenon and often referred to by many expressions as
atmosphere, surrounding milieu, environment and culture etc.
Every organization has its own traditions, methods of action,

1.   Gangadhar Rao, M. Rao V.S.P. Narayana, P.S. Organizational
     Behaviour, Konark Publication, New Delhi, 1990, p.1.

culture, which in their totality comprise its climate for people. Organizational Climate is a very important factor to be considered in studying and analysing organizations because it has a profound influence on the outlook, well being and attitudes of organizational members and thus on their total performance. Organizational Climate provides a useful platform for understanding characteristics of organizations as stability, creativity and innovation, communication and effectiveness etc....[2]

2.2   WHAT IS ORGANIZATIONAL CLIMATE?

Although intangible organizational climate is a real phenomenon while a precise definition of climate may be lacking. This does not preclude its existence. In the literature of organizational behaviour several different definitions have been advanced and almost all have a greater degree of commonality.

In the view of Keith Davis, Organizational Climate is the human environment within which an organization's employees do their work. It may refer to the environment

---

2. Ibid., p.488.

within a department a major company unit such as a branch plant or an entire organization.[3] Pritchard and Karasick (1973) define organizational climate as a relatively enduring quality of the internal environment of an organization distinguishing it from other organisations which (a) results from the behaviour and policies of the top management, (b) is perceived by the members (c) serves as a basis for interpreting the situation, and (d) acts as a source of pressure for directing activity.

Organizational Climate is the summary perception which people have about an organization. It is, thus a global expression of what the organization is. This is the observation of Benjamin Schneider and Rover. A snyder.[4]

Organizational Climate is thus, the manifestation of the attitudes of organizational members toward the organization itself. An organization tends to attract and keep people who fit its climate, so that its patterns are perpetuated

3. Keith Davis, Human Behaviour at Work, Tata McGraw Hill Book Company, New Delhi, 1985, p.104.

4. Benjamin Schneider and Rover A. Snyder, "Some Relationships between job satisfaction and organizational climate", Journal of applied psychology, 1975, p.380.

at least to some extent. Organizational Climate can be seen
as the perceived properties or characteristics found in the
work environment that results largely from action taken con-
sciously or unconsciously by an organization and that persum-
ably affects subsequent behaviour.

2.3   ORGANIZATIONAL CLIMATE AND PSYCHOLOGICAL CLIMATE

Though Organizational Climate and psychological
climate are usually interchangeable, there is a distinction
between psychological climate and organizational climate.
If a study is confined to a single organization and the
climate scores are analysed using the individual as the
unit of analysis, it is called as study of psychological
climate.   If on the other hand, it is a multi organization
study and the climate scores from each organization are
totalled, averaged and analysed using the 'Organization' as
the unit of analysis, it is called as study of Organizational
Climate.

2.4   SIGNIFICANCE OF ORGANIZATIONAL CLIMATE

The available literature shows that climate is
important to the well being of an organization in many ways.

The concept of climate provides a frame work for conceptu-
alising motivations at a collective, rather than just the
individual level, typical of motivational moders in psychology (Schneider, 1981)[5]. The contexual features of an
organization representative of processes such as technology,
structure and management policies are persumed to affect
perceptions of climate. Organizational Climate helps to
maximise the value position as revealed in the concern for
higher operational efficiency, profitability short term and
long term gains to the organization and so on.

2.5 IMPACT OF ORGANIZATIONAL CLIMATE

Organizational Climate has a major influence on
human performance through its impact on individual motivation
and job satisfaction. It does this by creating certain kinds
of expectancies about the consequences that will follow from
different actions. Individuals in the organization have
certain expectations and fulfilment of these expectations
depends upon their perception as how the Organizational Climate
suits the satisfaction of their needs. Thus Organizational

---

5. Schneider, B. "Individual Performance and Organizational
   Realities", Journal of Applied Psychology, 1972, pp.211-217.

Climate provides a type of work environment in which individua
feels satisfied or dissatisfied. Since satisfaction of
individual goes a long way in determining his efficiency,
Organizational Climate can be said to be directly related
with his performance in the organization.

There are four mechanisms by which Organizational
Climate affects performance, satisfaction and attitudes of
people in the organization. First, organizational variables
can operate as constraint system in both a positive and negat
sense by providing knowledge of what kinds of behaviour are
rewarded, punished or ignored. The organization can influenc
behaviour by attaching different rewards and punishment to
varying behaviours. Second, organizational variables may
affect behaviour through evaluation of the self and others,
and such evaluation will, in turn, influence behaviour. There
are both physiological and psychological variables associated
with this evaluation process. Third, organizational factors
work as stimuli. As stimuli they influence an individual's
arousal level, which is a motivational variable directing
behaviour. These level of arousal will directly affect the
level of activation and hence performance. Fourth, Organizational variables influence the individual to form a percepti

of the organization. This perception then influences
behaviour. Thus, Organizational Climate influences. The
way an individual in the organization behaves. This climate
consists of total organizational factors, including its
authority pattern, leadership pattern, and communication
pattern, three aspects discussed earlier as a means of
influencing behaviour.[6]

2.6   ORGANIZATIONAL CLIMATE AND JOB SATISFACTION

Job satisfaction is an integral component of
Organizational Climate and an important element in management
employee relationship. Job satisfaction is a positive
emotional state that occurs when a person's job seems to fulfil
important job values. Provided these values are compatible
with one's needs. Job satisfaction in simple words is an
individual's emotional relation to the job itself. It is a
person's attitude towards the job. People spend a sizable
amount of their time in work environment. From any minimally
humanitarian point of view, they expect that portion of their
lives to be more or less pleasant agreeable, satisfying and

---

6. Prasad, L.M., Organisation Theory and Behaviour, Sultan
    Chand & Sons, New Delhi, 1984, p.378.

fulfilling. Job satisfaction has been the centre of concentration for researchers over three decades. The reasons for such concentration are many fold job satisfaction has some relation with mental health of the people; job satisfaction has some degree of positive correlation with physical health of individuals. It spreads good will about the organization and it reduces absentism and increases turnover.

2.7 ORGANIZATIONAL CLIMATE AND MORALE

Morale is the vital ingredient of organizational success for it reflects the attitudes and sentiments the individual or group has toward the organizational objectives. These feelings and sentiments largely affect the productivity and satisfaction of individuals. When people are enthusiastic in their work environment we generally label them to be having "high morale". Dale S. Beach observed that Morale is the total satisfaction a person derives from his job, his work group his boss, his organization and his environment.[7] Morale is frequently referred to as being satisfaction and happiness of people. Morale is involved in everything that makes job satisfying.

---

7. Andrew Dubrin, Personnel and Human Resources Management, MacMillan Publishing Company, New York, 1981, p.236.

High Morale is the hall mark of sound behavioural
climate in the organization. Low morale results in ineffi-
ciency, waste and industrial indiscipline. The factors
affecting morale of employees in a work organization can be
external factors like personality of the employee, psychological make up, level of intelligence, physical health, family
background, relations with social groups and friends, and
internal factors like organizational goals, organizational
structure, nature of work, working conditions, Management
philosophies, compensation and groups. So, Morale is the
another name for Organizational Climate.[8]

2.8   FACTORS IN ORGANIZATIONAL CLIMATE.

From the available literature, researchers on
Organizational Climate have used data relating to individual
perception of organizational properties in identifying
Organizational Climate with great amount of diversity. The
results of various researchers and results of these studies
show that it is very difficult to generalise the basic
contents of Organizational Climate based on these studies.
Some broad generalizations can be drawn and it can be concluded that the following factors are some what common to
the findings of most studies.

---

8. Gangadhar Rao, V.S.P., Narayana, P.S., Op.cit., pp.495-496.

2.8.1   Organizational Context

Management philosophy is the foremost influential
factor that affects the climate. If an organization wedded
to such a policy effectively utilizes its resources both
human as well as non human. Then it can be concluded that
the climate is good. The man power philosophy is generally
expressed by rules, regulations and policies etc. The point
here is that the reactions of the employees and the degrees
to which they welcome and accept the managerial philosophy
is crucial to the development of sound and favourable organizational Climate.   The climate is said to be highly favourable when the existing management techniques are such that
employees goals are perfectly matched to the ideals of
organization.

2.8.2   Organizational Structure

Structure of the organization represents another
variable that affects climate. It needs no reiteration
that structure is a framework that establishes formal
relationships and delineate authority and functional responsibility. A management that has a strong belief in parti-
cipative decision-making will promote decentralization.
In a sharp contrast, if the management feels the necessity

of maintaining greater degree of consistency in operations regarding decision-making, it will be wedded to centralized structure. Thus structure also affects the climate of organizations.

2.8.3 Process

In every organization certain processes are vital so that it runs. Communication decision making, motivation and leadership are some of the very important processes through which the management carrier out its objectives. In all these processes, the relationship between superior and sub-ordinate is visible and therefore the supervisor cannot afford to ignore this visible interface. For instance, if we consider leader-follower relationship in leadership process, it is leader's choice whether to allow sub ordinates in decision-making give assignments, do performance appraisal etc. A leader has to be aware of the possible influence of his action on climate when deciding about the most appropriate supervisory technique for a given situation. It should be noted that failure to give consideration to the effect on climate would be monumental error that could be reflected adversely on the performance of employees. Further more, when a leader mismatches his style to the situation it might about any hope of attaining organizational objectives.

2.8.4   Physical Environment

The external conditions of environment, the size
and location of the building in which an employee works,
the size of the city, weather or the place all affect the
organizational climate.   An employee performing his job in
a relatively clean, quiet and safe environment will undoubt-
edly have a favourable perception of the Organizational
Climate.

2.8.5   System Values and Norms

The formal value system is communicated to
employees through rules regulations and policies. Although
in every organization informal organization also exists;
the value system of informal organization is difficult to
ascertain.   But from the point of view of Organizational
Climate, both formal and informal groups are very powerful
in exerting influence on climate. For instance, the organization that treats employees with respect to understanding
will have certainly a different climate than the one which
is very cold and impersonal.

2.9 ORGANIZATIONAL CLIMATE AND EMPLOYEE PERFORMANCE

Employee performance refers to an act of fulfilment of the requirements of a given job ie., the manner in which an employee carries out his job his efficiency at work or accomplishment and discharge of duty. Since climate is also generally regarded as existing at the individual or group level (as opposed to an organization-wide level), out come measures must also be considered at the individual or group level. Where climate is conducive to the needs of individuals, we would expect a high level of goal oriented behaviour. Conversely where the emerging climate is in opposition to personal goals, needs and motives, we can expect both performance and satisfaction to be low. Relationship between Organizational Climate and employee performance has been examined by many researchers. Various research studies confirm the positive relationship between organizational Climate and employee performance. Pritchard and Karasick (1973) have observed that Organizational Climate is fairly strongly related to subunit performance and job satisfaction.

2.10 CONCLUSION

Organizational Climate is a relatively enduring quality of the internal environment of an organization as

perceived and experienced by members which can be described
in terms of specific dimensions or characteristics and which
influences the patterns of behaviour and work performance of
others.

Job satisfaction and morale of the employees and
workers have close relationship with Organizational Climate.
Without having conducive climate to work it will result in
poor growth, poor sales, lock out and strikes.   Factors
influencing Organizational Climate, different dimensions of
Organizational Climate have been studied in this chapter.

CHAPTER III

EMPLOYEES ATTITUDE TOWARDS ORGANIZATIONAL CLIMATE

PERTAINING TO PERSONAL FACTORS

3.1   INTRODUCTION

Organizational Climate has different dimensions.
Attitude of the workers towards the dimensions of Organizational Climate in selected units have been presented in
this chapter.   Personal factors influencing the Organizational Climate have been analysed.   The primary data
collected from the respondents have been used to measure
the attitude of the workers and the personal factors influencing the different Organizational dimensions.

3.2   SCORING SCHEME

In the Interview Schedule, Organizational Climate
has been analysed through seven dimensions.   In each
dimension seven statements were given.   Those who strongly
agree with the statement are allotted 5 marks, those who
agree with the statement are allotted 4 marks, those who
offer no opinion about the given statement are allotted 3
marks; those who disagree with the statement are allotted
2 marks and those who strongly disagree with the statement
are allotted 1 mark.

The respondents are classified into three levels.

i) Respondent who rated the Organizational Climate as good.

ii) Respondent who rated the Organizational Climate as moderate.

iii) Respondent who rated the Organizational Climate as not good.

For the above classification the following steps have been used.

In the Interview Schedule, 49 statements were given. So a maximum of 245 marks can be scored by a respondent. The total number of respondents is 101 in Melur unit and 52 in Andipatti unit.

$$\text{Arithmatic Mean} = \frac{\leq X}{N}$$

$\leq X$ = Total score of the respondents

$\leq f \, X$ = Mean deviation of respondent

In Melur Unit

$$\text{Arithmatic Mean} = \frac{\leq X}{N}$$

$$= \frac{15236}{101}$$

$$= 150.85$$

$$\text{Standard deviation} = \sqrt{\frac{\leq f x^2}{n}}$$

$$= \sqrt{\frac{58223}{101}}$$

$$= 24.01$$

Respondents who rated the Organizational Climate as Good. Score will be more than

| 150.85 | + | 24.01 | = 174.86 (or) 175 |
| (Arithmatic Mean) | | (Standard deviation) | |

Respondents who rated the Organizational Climate as Not Good - Score will be lower than.

150.85	-	24.01	=	126.84	(or)	127
(Arithmatic mean)		(Standard deviation)				

Respondents who obtained scores between good and not good have been classified as ones rated Organizational Climate as Moderate.

In Andipatti Unit
_____

$$\text{Arithmatic Mean} = \frac{\leq X}{N}$$

$$= \frac{7394}{52}$$

$$= 142.192$$

$$\text{Standard deviation} = \sqrt{\frac{\leq f x^2}{N}}$$

$$= \sqrt{\frac{26133.782}{52}}$$

$$= 22.418$$

Respondents who rated the Organizational Climate as GOOD - Score will be more than

142.92   +   22.418   = 165.338   (or)   165

(Arithmatic   (Standard
   Mean)   deviation)

Respondents who rated the Organizational Climate as NOT GOOD - Score will be lower than.

142.92   -   22.418   = 120.502   (or)   121

(Arithmatic   (Standard
   Mean)   deviation)

Respondents who obtained scores between Good and Not Good have been classified as ones who rated Organizational Climate as"Moderate".

This calculation is also applied in every dimension of Organizational Climate to classify it into good, moderate and not good.   On the basis of the above classification, chi-square test has been applied to test the hypotheses.

3.3 EXTENT OF ORGANIZATIONAL CLIMATE

Table 3.1 shows the attitude level of the respondents towards Organizational Climate.

TABLE 3.1

Attitude Level of Respondent

Category	Melur	Andipatti
Good	12 (11.88%)	9(17.31%)
Moderate	79 (78.22%)	33(63.46%)
Not Good	10 (9.9%)	10(19.23%)
Total	101 (100%)	52(100%)

Table 3.1 indicates that out of 101 respondents
in Melur unit, 79(78.22%) have rated Organizational Climate
as Moderate.   In Andipatti unit, out of 52 respondents
33(63.46%) have rated Organizational Climate as Moderate.
It is, therefore concluded that the workers attitude towards
Organizational Climate in both the mills has to be rated as
"Moderate".

3.4   FACTORS INFLUENCING THE ORGANIZATIONAL CLIMATE

In order to study the personal factors influencing the Organizational Climate, the following hypotheses have been framed.

1.   Organizational Climate has association with the age of the employee.

2.   The educational qualification of the employees has association with Organizational Climate.

3.   The social group of the employee influences the attitude of the employee towards Organizational Climate.

In order to verify the hypotheses, all the seven dimensions are analysed separately.

3.4.1   The Age of the Employees has Association with their Attitude towards Organizational Climate

TABLE 3.2

Age of the Employee and their
Average Mean Score

Age of Employee	Melur		Andipatti	
	No. of Employees	Average Mean Score	No. of Employee	Average Mean Score
Upto 25	-	-	14	149.724
26 - 35	22	123.201	30	160.561
36 - 45	59	147.828	8	119.121
46 and above	20	173.721	-	-
Total	101		52	

Table 3.2 shows that, in Melur unit, the employees
belonging to age group of 46 and above have more favourable
attitude towards the Organizational Climate. At the same time,
In Andipatti Unit, the employees belonging to the age group
of 26-35 have more favourable attitude towards Organizational
Climate.

In order to test whether there is significant
correlation between the age group of employee and their
attitude towards Organizational Climate. Chi-square test
has been applied to all the dimensions.

Null Hypothesis : Age of the employees and their attitude
towards workers attitude are independent
in Melur.

TABLE 3.3

Age of the Employees and their Attitude towards
Workers Attitude-in Melur x^2 - Test

O	E	O-E	$(O-E)^2$	$\dfrac{(O-E)^2}{E}$
12	16.923	-4.923	24.236	1.4321
18	23.366	-5.366	28.794	1.232
10	7.921	2.079	4.322	0.546
8	12.198	-4.198	17.623	1.445
39	32.713	6.287	39.526	1.208
9	11.089	-2.089	4.364	0.394
2	1.089	0.911	0.830	0.762
2	2.921	-0.921	0.848	0.290
1	0.990	-0.010	0.001	0.001
			Total	7.310

Degree of Freedom = 4

Calculated x^2 value = 7.310

Table x^2 value at 5% level 9.488

Table 3.3 indicates that the calculated chi-square value is lesser than the table value at 5% level and hence the chi-square test reveals that the age group of employees, in in Melur unit has/significant relationship with their attitude towards workers attitude.

Null Hypothesis : Age of the employees and their attitude towards workers attitude are independent in Andipatti

TABLE 3.4

Age of the Employees and their Attitude towards Workers Attitude-Andipatti X^2 - Test

O	E	O-E	$(O-E)^2$	$\dfrac{(O-E)^2}{E}$
7	4.038	2.962	8.773	2.173
5	8.077	-3.077	9.468	1.172
2	1.885	0.115	0.013	0.001
6	9.231	-3.231	10.439	1.131
22	18.461	3.539	12.524	0.678
4	4.308	-0.308	0.094	0.022
2	1.731	0.269	0.723	0.418
3	3.462	-0.462	0.213	0.062
1	0.807	0.193	0.037	0.046
			Total	5.703

Degree of Freedom   =   4

Calculated X^2 value   =   5.703

Table X^2 value at 5% level   9.488

    Table 3.4 indicates that the calculated chi-square value is less than the table value at 5% level and hence the chi-square test reveals that the relationship between the age of the employees and their attitude towards workers attitude in Andipatti is insignificant.

Null Hypothesis : Age of the employees and their attitude
towards job characteristics in Melur is
independent.

TABLE 3.5

Age of the Employees and their Attitude towards
Job Characteristice-Melur X^2 - Test

O	E	O-E	$(O-E)^2$	$\dfrac{(O-E)^2}{E}$
8	5.663	2.337	5.612	0.964
9	15.188	-6.188	38.291	2.521
9	5.149	3.851	14.830	2.880
12	14.811	-2.811	7.902	0.534
47	39.724	9.276	86.044	2.166
19	13.465	5.535	30.636	2.775
2	1.525	0.475	0.226	0.147
3	4.089	-1.089	11.859	0.290
2	1.386	0.614	0.377	0.272
			Total	12.049

Degree of Freedom = 4

Calculated x^2 value = 12.049

Table x^2 value at 5% level 9.488

Table 3.5 indicates that the calculated chi-square value is higher than the table value at 5% level and hence the chi-square test reveals that the relationship between the age of the employees and their attitude towards job characteristics is significant.

Null Hypothesis : Age of the employees and their attitude towards job characteristics is independent in Andipatti.

TABLE 3.6

Age of the Employees and their Attitude towards
Job Characteristics-In Andipatti X^2-Test

O	E	O-E	$(O-E)^2$	$\dfrac{(O-E)^2}{E}$
11	10.962	0.038	1.444	0.132
24	21.923	2.077	4.313	0.197
3	5.115	-2.115	4.473	0.874
3	2.019	0.981	0.962	0.476
2	4.038	-2.038	4.153	1.028
2	0.943	1.057	1.117	1.185
1	2.019	-1.019	1.038	0.514
.4	4.039	-0.039	1.521	0.377
2	0.942	1.058	1.119	1.188
			Total	5.971

Degree of Freedom   = 4

Calculated X^2 value   = 5.971

Table X^2 value at 5% level 9.488

      Table 3.6 indicates that the calculated chi-square value is less than the table value at 5% level and hence the chi-square test reveals that the relationship between the age of the employees and their attitude towards job characteristics in Andipatti is insignificant.

Null Hypothesis : Age of the employees and their attitude

towards working conditions is independent

in Melur.

TABLE 3.7

Age of the Employees and their Attitude towards
Working Conditions - In Melur

x^2 - Test

O	E	O-E	$(O-E)^2$	$\dfrac{(O-E)^2}{E}$
2	2.396	-0.396	0.157	0.065
2	6.426	-4.426	19.589	3.048
1	2.178	-1.178	1.388	0.637
8	13.069	-5.069	25.695	1.966
44	35.050	8.950	80.103	2.285
8	11.881	-3.881	15.062	1.268
12	6.534	5.466	29.877	4.573
13	17.525	-4.525	20.476	1.168
5	5.941	-0.941	0.885	0.149
			Total	15.159

Degree of Freedom = 4

Calculated x^2 value = 15.159

Table x^2 value at 5% level of 9.488

Table 3.7 indicates that the calculated chi-square value is higher than the table value at 5% level and hence the chi-square test reveals that the relationship between the age of the employees and their attitude towards working conditions in Melur is significant.

Null Hypothesis : Age of the employees and their attitude towards working conditions is independent in Andipatti.

TABLE 3.8

Age of the Employees and their Attitude towards Working Conditions - In Andipatti

x^2 - Test

O	E	O-E	$(O-E)^2$	$\frac{(O-E)^2}{E}$
0	0.865	-0.865	0.748	0.865
1	1.731	-0.731	0.534	0.308
2	0.404	1.596	2.547	6.304
7	7.211	-0.211	0.044	0.001
16	14.423	1.577	2.486	0.172
2	3.365	-1.365	1.863	0.554
8	6.924	1.026	1.052	0.152
13	13.846	-0.846	0.715	0.052
3	3.231	-0.231	0.053	0.016
			Total	8.424

Degree of Freedom   =   4

Calculated x^2 value =   8.424

Table x^2 value at 5% level   9.488

      Table 3.8 indicates that the calculated chi-square value is lower than the table value at 5% level and hence the chi-square test reveals that the relationship between the age of the employees and their attitude towards working conditions in Andipatti is insignificant.

Null Hypothesis : Age of the employees and their attitude towards personnel policies is independent in Melur.

TABLE 3.9

Age of the Employees and their Attitude towards Personnel Policies - In Melur

X^2 - Test

O	E	O-E	$(O-E)^2$	$\dfrac{(O-E)^2}{E}$
0	1.089	-1.089	1.186	1.089
4	2.921	1.079	1.164	0.399
1	0.990	0.010	0.001	0.001
5	9.149	-4.149	17.214	1.882
30	24.535	5.465	29.866	1.217
7	8.316	-1.316	1.732	0.208
17	11.762	5.238	27.437	2.333
25	31.545	6.545	42.837	1.358
12	10.693	1.307	1.708	0.160
			Total	8.647

Degree of Freedom = 4

Calculated X^2 value = 8.647

Table X^2 value at 5% level 9.488

Table 3.9 indicates that the calculated chi-square
value is lower than the table value at 5% level and hence
the chi-square test reveals that the relationship between
the age of the employees and their attitude towards personnel
policies in Melur is insignificant.

Null Hypothesis : Age of the employees and their attitude
towards personnel policies is independent
in Andipatti

TABLE 3.10

Age of the Employees and their Attitude towards
Personnel Policies - In Andipatti
X^2 - Test

O	E	O-E	$(O-E)^2$	$\dfrac{(O-E)^2}{E}$
5	5.193	-0.193	0.037	0.001
10	10.381	-0.381	0.145	0.014
3	2.424	+0.576	0.331	0.137
10	9.808	0.192	0.036	0.001
20	19.616	0.384	0.147	0.001
4	4.578	-0.578	0.334	0.073
			Total	0.227

Degree of Freedom = 2
Calculated X^2 value = 0.227
Table X^2 value at 5% level 5.991

Table 3.10 indicates that the calculated chi-square value is less than the table value at 5% level and hence the chi-square test reveals that the relationship between the age of the employees and their attitude towards personnel policies in Andipatti is insignificant.

Null Hypothesis :   Age of the employees and their attitude
                        towards performance reward relationship
                        is independent in Melur.

TABLE 3.11

Age of the Employees and their Attitude towards
Performance Reward Relationship-In Melur
x^2 - Test

O	E	O-E	$(O-E)^2$	$\dfrac{(O-E)^2}{E}$
0	0.653	-0.653	0.426	0.653
1	1.752	-0.752	0.566	0.323
2	0.595	1.405	1.974	3.318
10	6.751	3.249	10.556	1.564
12	18.901	-6.901	47.624	2.519
9	6.138	2.862	8.191	1.354
12	14.594	-2.594	6.729	0.461
46	39.139	6.861	47.073	1.203
9	13.267	-4.267	18.207	1.372
			Total	12.747

Degree of Freedom = 4

Calculated x^2 value = 12.747

Table x^2 value at 5% level 9.488

Table 3.11 indicates that the calculated chi-square value is higher than the table value at 5% level and hence the chi-square test reveals that there is significant relationship between the age of the employees and their attitude towards performance reward relationship in Melur.

Null Hypothesis : Age of the employees and their attitude towards performance reward relationship is independent in Andipatti.

TABLE 3.12

Age of the Employees and their Attitude towards Performance Reward Relationship-in Andipatti

x^2 - Test

O	E	O-E	$(O-E)^2$	$\dfrac{(O-E)^2}{E}$
0	0.288	-0.288	0.083	0.288
0	0.577	-0.577	0.333	0.577
1	0.135	0.865	0.748	5.541
4	4.330	-0.330	0.109	0.025
9	8.654	0.346	0.120	0.014
2	2.019	-0.019	0.001	0.001
11	10.384	0.616	0.379	0.036
21	20.768	0.232	0.053	0.001
4	4.845	-0.845	0.714	0.147
			Total	6.630

Degree of Freedom = 4

Calculated x^2 value = 6.630

Table x^2 value at 5% level 9.488

Table 3.12 indicates that the calculated chi-square
value is less than the table value at 5% level and hence the
chi-square test reveals that the relationship between the age
of the employees and their attitude towards performance
reward relationship in Andipatti is insignificant.

Null Hypothesis :   Age of the employees and their attitude
                    towards supervision is independent in
                    Melur.

TABLE 3.13

Age of the Employees and their Attitude towards
Supervision - In Melur
X^2 - Test

O	E	O-E	$(O-E)^2$	$\dfrac{(O-E)^2}{E}$
3	3.485	-0.485	0.235	0.067
6	9.347	-3.347	11.202	1.198
7	3.168	3.832	11.446	3.613
16	16.772	-0.772	0.596	0.035
49	44.980	4.020	16.160	0.359
12	15.248	-3.248	10.549	0.692
3	1.743	1.257	1.580	0.906
4	4.673	-0.673	0.453	0.096
1	1.584	-0.584	0.341	0.215
			Total	7.181

Degree of Freedom   =   4

Calculated X^2 value   =   7.181

Table X^2 value at 5% level   9.488

        Table 3.13 indicates that the calculated chi-square value is less than the table value at 5% level and hence the chi-square test reveals that the relationship between the age of the employees and their attitude towards supervision in Melur is insignificant.

Null Hypothesis : Age of the employees and their attitude
towards supervision is independent in
Andipatti.

TABLE 3.14

Age of the Employees and their Attitude towards
Supervision - In Andipatti
x^2 - Test

O	E	O-E	$(O-E)^2$	$\dfrac{(O-E)^2}{E}$
1	1.442	-0.442	0.195	0.135
2	2.885	-0.885	0.783	0.271
2	0.673	1.327	1.761	2.617
11	10.673	-0.327	0.107	0.010
24	21.346	-2.654	7.044	0.330
2	4.981	-2.981	8.886	1.784
3	2.885	-0.115	0.013	0.001
4	5.769	-1.1769	3.129	0.542
3	1.346	-1.654	2.738	0.492
			Total	6.182

Degree of Freedom   = 4

Calculated x^2 value   = 6.182

Table x^2 value at 5% level 9.488

Table 3.14 indicates that the calculated chi-square value is less than the table value at 5% level and hence the chi-square test reveals that the relationship between the age of the employees and their attitude towards supervision in Andipatti is insignificant.

Null Hypothesis : Age of the employees and their attitude towards communication is independent in Melur.

TABLE 3.15

Age of the Employees and their Attitude towards Communication - In Melur

X^2 - Test

O	E	O-E	$(O-E)^2$	$\frac{(O-E)^2}{E}$
2	3.267	-1.267	1.605	0.491
7	8.763	-1.763	3.108	0.555
6	2.970	3.030	9.181	3.091
16	15.901	0.099	0.001	0.001
45	42.644	2.356	5.551	0.130
12	14.455	-2.455	6.027	0.417
4	2.832	1.168	1.364	0.482
7	7.594	-0.594	0.353	0.046
2	2.574	0.574	0.329	0.128
			Total	5.341

Degree of Freedom   =   4

Calculated X^2 value   =   5.341

Table X^2 value at 5% level   9.488

      Table 3.15 indicates that the calculated chi-square value is less than the table value at 5% level and hence the chi-square test reveals that the relationship between the age of the employees and their attitude towards communication in Melur is insignificant.

Null Hypothesis : Age of the employees and their attitude
towards communication is independent in
Andipatti.

TABLE 3.16

Age of the Employees and their Attitude towards
Communication - In Andipatti
x^2 - Test

O	E	O-E	$(O-E)^2$	$\dfrac{(O-E)^2}{E}$
0	0.577	-0.577	0.333	0.577
1	1.154	-0.154	0.024	0.021
1	0.269	0.731	0.534	5.085
11	8.654	2.346	5.504	0.636
15	17.308	-2.308	5.327	0.308
4	4.038	-0.038	0.001	0.001
4	5.770	-1.770	3.133	0.543
14	11.538	2.462	6.061	0.525
2	2.692	-0.692	0.479	0.178
			Total	7.874

Degree of Freedom   =   4

Calculated x^2 value   =   7.874

Table x^2 value at 5% level 9.488

Table 3.16 indicates that the calculated chi-square value is less than the table value at 5% level and hence the chi-square test reveals that the relationship between the age of the employees and their attitude towards communication in Andipatti is insignificant.

Null Hypothesis : Age of the employees and their attitude towards Organizational Climate is independent in Melur.

TABLE 3.17

Age of the Employees and their Attitude towards Organizational Climate - In Melur

x^2 - Test

O	E	O-E	$(O-E)^2$	$\dfrac{(O-E)^2}{E}$
3	2.614	0.386	0.149	0.057
15	17.208	-2.208	4.875	0.283
4	2.178	1.822	3.319	1.524
4	7.010	-3.010	9.060	1.292
52	46.149	5.851	34.234	0.742
3	5.842	-2.842	8.077	1.383
5	2.375	-2.625	6.891	2.901
12	15.644	-3.644	13.279	0.849
3	1.980	1.020	1.040	0.525
			Total	9.556

Degree of Freedom   =   4

Calculated x^2 value   =   9.556

Table x^2 value at 5% level   9.488

         Table 3.17 indicates that the calculated chi-square value is higher than the table at 5% level and hence the chi-square test reveals that the relationship between the age of the employees and their attitude towards Organizational Climate in Melur is significant.

Null Hypothesis : Age of the employees and their attitude towards Organizational Climate is independent in Andipatti.

TABLE 3.18

Age of the Employees and their Attitude towards Organizational Climate - In Andipatti

X^2 - Test

O	E	O-E	$(O-E)^2$	$\dfrac{(O-E)^2}{E}$
2	2.077	0.077	0.001	0.001
5	7.615	-2.615	6.838	0.898
5	2.308	2.692	7.247	3.139
3	5.192	-2.192	4.805	0.925
25	19.038	5.692	35.545	1.867
2	5.769	-3.769	14.205	2.462
4	1.731	2.269	5.148	2.974
3	6.347	-3.347	11.202	1.765
3	1.923	1.077	1.160	0.603
			Total	14.634

Degree of Freedom = 4

Calculated X^2 value = 14.634

Table X^2 value at 5% level 9.488

Table 3.18 indicates that the calculated chi-square value is higher than the table at 5% level and hence the chi-square test reveals that the relationship between the age of the employees and their attitude towards Organizational Climate in Andipatti is significant.

From the above tests the following conclusions have been drawn.

The age of the employees and their attitude towards workers attitude is significant in Melur and insignificant in Andipatti.

The age of the employees and their attitude towards job characteristics is significant in Melur and insignificant in Andipatti.

The age of the employees and their attitude towards working conditions is significant in Melur and insignificant in Andipatti.

The age of the employees and their attitude towards personnel policies is insignificant in both Melur and Andipatti.

The age of the employees and their attitude towards performance Reward Relationship is significant in Melur and insignificant in Andipatti.

The age of the employees and their attitude towards supervision is insignificant in both Melur and Andipatti.

The age of the employees and their attitude towards communication is insignificant in both Melur and Andipatti.

The age of the employees and their attitude towards Organizational Climate is significant in both Andipatti and Melur. Hence, the hypothesis the age of the employee influences the Organizational Climate - has been accepted.

3.4.2 Educational Qualification of the Employees has Association with their Attitude towards Organizational Climate

TABLE 3.19

Education of the Employees and their
Average Mean Score

Educational Qualification of Employee	Melur		Andipatti	
	No. of Employees	Average Mean Score	No. of Employees	Average Mean Score
School	86	128.466	36	134.763
Diploma	7	183.146	7	160.291
Degree and above	8	133.138	9	134.522
Total	101		52	

Table 3.19 shows that in both Melur and Andipatti units the employees belonging to the group of diploma have more favourable attitude towards Organizational Climate. In both the units, the degree holders and those who have educational qualification upto school level consider that the Organizational Climate is not good. In order to find out whether there is significant relationship between the educatio of the employees and their attitude towards Organizational Climate, chi-square test has been applied to all dimensions.

Null Hypothesis : Education of the employees and their
attitude towards workers attitude is
independent in Melur

TABLE 3.20

Education of the Employees and their Attitude towards
Workers Attitude - In Melur
x^2 - Test

O	E	O-E	$(O-E)^2$	$\dfrac{(O-E)^2}{E}$
32	34.060	-2.060	4.244	0.125
4	2.772	1.228	1.508	0.544
4	3.168	0.832	0.692	0.218
52	47.683	4.317	18.636	0.391
1	3.881	-2.881	8.300	2.139
3	4.436	-1.436	2.062	0.465
2	4.257	-2.257	5.094	1.197
2	0.347	1.653	2.732	7.874
1	0.396	0.604	0.365	0.921
			Total	13.874

Degree of Freedom = 4

Calculated x^2 value = 13.874

Table x^2 value at 5% level 9.488

Table 3.20 indicates that the calculated chi-square value is higher than the table value at 5% level and hence the chi-square test reveals that the relationship between the education of the employees and their attitude towards workers attitude is significant in Melur.

Null Hypothesis : Education of the employees and their attitude towards workers attitude is independent in Andipatti.

TABLE 3.21

Education of the Employees and their Attitude towards Workers Attitude - In Andipatti

X^2 - Test

O	E	O-E	$(O-E)^2$	$\dfrac{(O-E)^2}{E}$
9	9.692	0.692	0.479	0.049
2	1.885	0.115	0.013	0.001
3	2.423	0.577	0.333	0.137
26	22.154	3.846	14.792	0.668
2	4.308	-2.308	5.327	1.236
4	5.538	-1.538	2.365	0.427
1	4.154	-3.154	9.948	2.395
3	0.808	2.192	4.805	5.947
2	1.038	1.962	3.849	3.708
			Total	14.568

Degree of Freedom   =   4

Calculated x^2 value   = 14.568

Table x^2 value at 5% level 9.488

       Table 3.21 indicates that the calculated x^2 value is higher than the table value at 5% level and hence the chi-square test reveals that the relationship between the education of the employees and their attitude towards workers attitude is significant in Andipatti.

Null Hypothesis : Education of the employees and their
attitude towards job characteristics
is independent in Melur

TABLE 3.22

Education of the Employees and their Attitude towards
Job Characteristics - In Melur
x^2 - Test

O	E	O-E	$(O-E)^2$	$\dfrac{(O-E)^2}{E}$
21	22.139	-1.139	1.297	0.059
2	1.802	0.198	0.039	0.022
3	2.059	0.941	0.885	0.430
62	57.901	4.099	16.802	0.290
3	4.713	-1.713	2.934	0.623
3	5.386	-2.386	5.693	1.057
3	5.960	-2.960	8.762	1.470
2	0.485	1.515	2.295	4.732
2	0.555	1.445	2.089	3.762
			Total	12.445

Degree of Freedom   = 4

Calculated x^2 value   = 12.445

Table x^2 value at 5% level 9.488

Table 3.22 indicates that the calculated x^2 value is higher than the table value at 5% level and hence the chi-square test reveals that the relationship between the education of the employees and their attitude towards job characteristics is significant in Melur.

Null Hypothesis : Education of the employees and their attitude towards job characteristics is independent in Andipatti.

TABLE 3.23

Education of the Employees and their Attitude towards Job Characteristics - In Andipatti

x^2 - Test

O	E	O-E	$(O-E)^2$	$\frac{(O-E)^2}{E}$
29	26.308	2.692	7.247	0.275
3	5.115	-2.115	4.473	0.875
6	6.577	-0.577	0.333	0.051
3	4.846	-1.846	3.408	0.703
2	0.942	1.058	1.119	1.188
2	1.212	0.788	0.608	0.502
4	4.846	-0.846	0.716	0.148
2	0.942	1.058	1.119	0.188
1	1.212	0.212	0.045	0.037
			Total	4.967

Degree of Freedom $= 4$

Calculated X^2 value $= 14.967$

Table X^2 value at 5% level 9.488

Table 3.23 indicates that the calculated X^2 value is less than the table value at 5% level and hence the chi-square test reveals that the relationship between the education of the employees and their attitude towards job characteristics is insignificant in Andipatti.

Null Hypothesis :   Education of the employees and their

attitude towards working conditions

is independent in Melur.

TABLE 3.24

Education of the Employees and their Attitude towards
Working Conditions - In Melur
x^2 - Test

O	E	O-E	$(O-E)^2$	$\frac{(O-E)^2}{E}$
25	25.545	-0.545	0.297	0.012
4	2.079	1.921	3.690	1.775
1	2.376	-1.376	1.893	0.797
55	51.089	3.911	15.296	0.299
1	4.159	-3.159	9.979	2.399
4	4.752	-0.752	0.566	0.119
6	9.366	-3.366	11.329	1.207
2	0.763	1.237	1.530	2.005
3	0.871	2.129	4.533	5.204
			Total	13.817

Degree of Freedom   = 4

Calculated x^2 value   = 13.817

Table x^2 value at 5% level 9.488

Table 3.24 indicates that the calculated x^2 value
is higher than the table value at 5% level and hence the
chi-square test reveals that the relationship between the
education of the employees and their attitude towards
working conditions is significant in Melur.

Null Hypothesis :   Education of the employees and their
attitude towards working conditions is
independent in Andipatti.

TABLE 3.25

Education of the Employees and their Attitude towards
Working Conditions - In Andipatti
x^2 - Test

O	E	O-E	$(O-E)^2$	$\dfrac{(O-E)^2}{E}$
2	2.077	-0.770	0.593	0.285
1	0.404	0.596	0.355	0.879
0	0.519	-0.519	0.269	0.519
18	17.308	0.692	0.479	0.028
3	3.365	-0.365	0.133	0.040
4	4.327	-0.327	0.107	0.025
16	16.615	-0.615	0.378	0.028
3	3.231	-0.231	0.053	0.017
5	4.154	0.846	0.716	0.172
			Total	1.993

Degree of Freedom   = 4

Calculated X^2 value   = 1.993

Table X^2 value at 5% level 9.488

      Table 3.25 indicates that the calculated X^2 value is less than the table value at 5% level and hence the chi-square test reveals that the relationship between the education of the employees and their attitude towards working conditions is insignificant in Andipatti.

Null Hypothesis : Education of the employees and their
attitude towards personnel policies
is independent in Melur.

TABLE 3.26

Education of the Employees and their Attitude towards
Personnel Policies - In Melur
x^2 - Test

O	E	O-E	$(O-E)^2$	$\dfrac{(O-E)^2}{E}$
3	4.257	-1.257	1.580	0.371
1	0.347	0.653	0.426	1.229
1	0.396	0.604	0.365	0.921
37	35.762	1.238	1.533	0.042
3	2.911	0.089	0.001	0.001
2	3.327	-1.327	1.761	0.529
46	45.980	0.020	0.001	0.001
3	3.743	-0.743	0.552	0.147
5	4.277	0.723	0.523	0.122
			Total	3.363

Degree of Freedom   = 4
Calculated x^2 value   = 3.363
Table x^2 value at 5% level 9.488

Table 3.26 indicates that the calculated x^2 value
is less than the table value at 5% level and hence the chi-
square test reveals that the relationship between the education
of the employees and their attitude towards personnel policies
is insignificant in Melur.

Null Hypothesis : Education of the employees and their

attitude towards personnel policies

is independent in Andipatti.

TABLE 3.27

Education of the Employees and their Attitude towards
Personnel Policies - In Andipatti
x^2 - Test

O	E	O-E	$(O-E)^2$	$\frac{(O-E)^2}{E}$
13	12.462	0.538	0.289	0.023
1	2.423	-1.423	2.025	0.836
4	3.115	0.885	0.783	0.251
23	23.538	-0.538	0.289	0.012
6	4.577	1.433	2.053	0.449
5	5.885	-0.885	0.783	0.133
			Total	1.704

Degree of Freedom   =   2

Calculated x^2 value   =   1.704

Table x^2 value at 5% level   5.991

        Table 3.27 indicates that the calculated x^2 value is less than the table value at 5% level and hence the chi-square test reveals that the relationship between the education of the employees and their attitude towards personnel policies is insignificant in Andipatti.

Null Hypothesis :   Education of the employees and their

attitude towards performance reward

relationship is independent in Melur.

TABLE 3.28

Education of the Employees and their Attitude towards
Performance Reward Relationship - In Melur
X^2 - Test

O	E	O-E	$(O-E)^2$	$\frac{(O-E)^2}{E}$
2	2.554	-0.554	0.307	0.120
1	0.278	0.722	0.521	1.875
0	0.238	-0.238	0.057	0.238
26	26.396	-0.396	0.157	0.001
2	2.149	-0.149	0.022	0.010
3	2.455	0.545	0.297	8.265
58	57.049	0.951	0.904	0.016
4	4.644	-0.644	0.415	0.089
5	5.307	-0.307	0.094	0.018
			Total	10.632

Degree of Freedom   = 4

Calculated X^2 value   = 10.632

Table X^2 value at 5% level 9.488

Table 3.28 indicates that the calculated X^2 value is higher than the table value at 5% level and hence the chi-square test reveals that the relationship between the education of the employees and their attitude towards performance reward relationship is significant in Melur.

Null Hypothesis : Education of the employees and their attitude towards performance reward relationship is independent in Andipatti.

TABLE 3.29

Education of the Employees and their Attitude towards
Performance Reward Relationship-In Andipatti
X^2 - Test

O	E	O-E	$(O-E)^2$	$\frac{(O-E)^2}{E}$
1	0.692	0.308	0.095	0.137
0	0.135	-0.135	0.018	0.135
0	0.173	-0.173	0.030	0.173
4	10.385	-6.385	40.768	3.926
4	2.019	1.981	3.924	1.944
7	2.596	4.404	19.395	7.471
31	24.923	6.077	36.930	1.482
3	4.846	-1.846	3.408	0.703
2	6.231	-4.231	17.901	2.873
			Total	18.844

Degree of Freedom   =   4

Calculated x^2 value   =   18.844

Table x^2 value at 5% level   9.488

      Table 3.29 indicates that the calculated x^2 value is higher than the table value at 5% level and hence the chi-square test reveals that the relationship between the education of the employees and their attitude towards performance reward relationship is significant in Andipatti.

Null Hypothesis : Education of the employees and their attitude towards supervision is independent in Melur.

TABLE 3.30

Education of the Employees and their Attitude towards Supervision - In Melur

x^2 - Test

O	E	O-E	$(O-E)^2$	$(\frac{O-E}{E})^2$
13	13.624	-0.624	0.389	0.029
1	1.109	-0.109	0.012	0.011
2	1.267	0.733	0.531	0.424
69	65.564	3.436	11.806	0.180
2	5.337	-3.337	11.136	2.086
6	6.099	-0.099	0.001	0.001
4	6.812	-2.812	7.907	1.161
4	0.554	3.446	11.875	21.435
0	0.634	-0.634	0.402	0.634
			Total	25.961

Degree of Freedom = 4

Calculated x^2 value = 25.961

Table x^2 value at 5% level 9.488

Table 3.30 indicates that the calculated x^2 value
is higher than the table value at 5% level and hence the chi-
square test reveals that the relationship between the education
of the employees and their attitude towards supervision is
significant in Melur.

Null Hypothesis : Education of the employees and
their attitude towards supervision
is independent in Andipatti.

TABLE 3.31

Education of the Employees and their Attitude towards
Supervision - In Andipatti
x^2 - Test

O	E	O-E	$(O-E)^2$	$\frac{(O-E)^2}{E}$
0	3.462	-3.462	11.985	3.462
2	0.673	1.327	1.530	2.274
3	0.865	2.135	4.558	5.270
30	25.615	4.385	119.228	5.136
2	4.981	-2.981	8.886	1.784
5	6.404	-1.404	1.971	0.308
6	6.923	-0.923	0.852	0.123
3	1.346	1.654	2.736	2.032
1	1.731	-0.731	6.534	0.309
			Total	20.698

Degree of Freedom   = 4

Calculated x^2 value   = 20.698

Table x^2 value at 5% level 9.488

       Table 3.31 indicates that the calculated x^2 value is higher than the table value at 5% level and hence the chi-square test reveals that the relationship between the education of the employees and their attitude towards supervision is significant in Andipatti.

Null Hypothesis : Education of the employees and their attitude towards communication is independent in Melur.

TABLE 3.32

Education of the Employees and their Attitude towards Communication - In Melur

x^2 - Test

O	E	O-E	$(O-E)^2$	$\dfrac{(O-E)^2}{E}$
3	12.772	-9.772	95.492	7.447
5	1.040	3.960	1.568	1.509
7	1.188	5.812	3.779	28.434
71	62.158	8.842	78.181	1.258
1	5.060	-4.060	16.484	3.258
1	5.782	-4.782	22.867	3.955
12	11.069	0.931	0.867	0.078
1	0.901	0.099	0.001	0.001
0	1.029	-1.029	1.059	1.029
			Total	46.998

Degree of Freedom = 4

Calculated x^2 value = 46.998

Table x^2 value at 5% level   9.488

Table 3.32 indicates that the calculated chi-square value is higher than the table value at 5% level and hence the chi-square test reveals that the relationship between the education of the employees and their attitude towards communication is significant in Melur.

Null Hypothesis : Education of the employees and their attitude towards communication is independent in Andipatti.

TABLE 3.33

Education of the Employees and their Attitude towards Communication - In Andipatti

x^2 - Test

O	E	O-E	$(O-E)^2$	$\frac{(O-E)^2}{E}$
0	1.385	-1.385	1.918	1.385
0	0.269	-0.269	0.072	0.269
2	0.346	1.654	2.736	7.907
18	20.770	-2.770	7.673	0.369
5	4.038	0.962	0.925	0.229
7	5.112	1.808	3.269	0.629
18	13.846	4.154	17.256	1.246
2	2.692	-0.692	0.479	0.178
20	3.462	-3.462	11.985	0.511
			Total	12.723

Degree of Freedom   =   4

Calculated X^2 value   =   12.723

Table X^2 value at 5% level   9.488

       Table 3.33 indicates that the calculated X^2 value is higher than the table value at 5% level and hence the chi-square test reveals that the relationship between the education of the employees and their attitude towards communication is significant in Andipatti.

Null Hypothesis : Education of employees and their
attitude towards Organizational
Climate is independent in Melur.

TABLE 3.34

Education of Employees and their Attitude towards
Organizational Climate - In Melur
x^2 - Test

O	E	O-E	$(O-E)^2$	$\frac{(O-E)^2}{E}$
9	10.218	-1.218	1.484	0.145
73	67.267	5.733	32.867	0.489
4	8.515	-4.515	20.385	2.394
2	0.832	1.168	1.364	1.640
2	5.475	-3.475	12.076	2.205
3	0.693	2.307	5.322	7.680
1	0.950	0.049	0.001	0.001
4	6.258	-2.258	5.099	0.815
3	0.792	-2.208	4.875	6.156
			Total	21.525

Degree of Freedom = 4
Calculated x^2 value = 21.525
Table x^2 value at 5% level 9.488

Table 3.34 indicates that the calculated x^2 value is higher than the table value at 5% level and hence the chi-square test reveals that the relationship between the education of employees and their attitude towards Organizational Climate is significant in Melur.

Null Hypothesis : Education of employees and their attitude towards Organizational Climate is independent in Andipatti.

TABLE 3.35

Education of Employees and their Attitude towards
Organizational Climate-In Andipatti
x^2 - Test

O	E	O-E	$(O-E)^2$	$\dfrac{(O-E)^2}{E}$
5	6.231	-1.231	1.515	0.243
27	22.846	4.154	17.256	0.755
4	6.923	-2.923	8.544	1.234
2	1.212	0.788	0.621	0.521
3	4.442	-1.442	2.079	0.468
2	1.346	0.654	0.428	0.318
2	1.556	0.442	0.195	0.125
3	5.711	-2.711	7.350	1.287
4	1.731	2.269	5.148	2.974
			Total	7.916

Degree of Freedom $= 4$

Calculated X^2 value $= 7.916$

Table X^2 value at 5% level 9.488

Table 3.35 indicates that the calculated X^2 value is less than the table value and hence, the chi-square test reveals that the relationship between the education of the employees and their attitude towards Organizational Climate is significant in Andipatti.

From the above tests the following conclusions have been drawn.

The education of the employees and their attitude towards workers attitude is significant in both Melur and Andipatti.

The education of the employees and their attitude towards job characteristics is significant in Melur and insignificant in Andipatti.

The education of the employees and their attitude towards working condition is significant is Melur and insignificant in Andipatti.

The education of the employees and their attitude
towards personnel policy is insignificant in both Melur and
Andipatti.

The education of the employees and their attitude
towards performance reward relationship is significant in
both Melur and Andipatti.

The education of the employees and their attitude
towards supervision is significant in both Melur and Andipatti.

The education of the employees and their attitude
towards communication is significant in both Melur and
Andipatti.

The education of the employees and their attitude
towards Organizational Climate is significant in Melur and
insignificant in Andipatti.

Hence, the hypothesis the education of employees
influences, their attitude towards Organizational Climate
is accepted in the case of Melur and rejected in the case of
Andipatti.

3.4.6   Social Group of the employee influences the attitude
of employee towards Organizational Climate

TABLE 3.36

Social Group of the Employees and their
Average Mean Score

Social Group of Employees	Melur		Andipatti	
	Number of Employees	Average Mean Score	Number of Employees	Average Mean Score
F.C.	16	154.776	9	164.297
B.C.	66	160.465	24	149.643
S.C/S.T.	19	129.509	19	115.636
Total	101		52	

Table 3.36 shows that in both Melur mill and Andipatti mill, employees who belong to scheduled caste have less
favourable attitude towards Organizational Climate. In
Andipatti mill the forward caste employees considered the
existing Organizational Climate to be good whereas the other
groups considered it to be not good. In Melur, the backward
class employees regarded the existing Organizational Climate
be good while the other groups. One of the opinion that it
is not good. Whether there is correlation between the social

group of employees and their attitude towards Organizational
Climate chi-square test has been applied.

Null Hypothesis : Social Group of employees and their
attitude towards workers attitude is
independent in Melur.

TABLE 3.37

Social Group of Employees and their Attitude towards
Workers Attitude - In Melur

X^2 - Test

O	E	O-E	$(O-E)^2$	$\dfrac{(O-E)^2}{E}$
6	6.337	-0.337	0.114	0.018
25	26.139	-1.139	1.297	0.050
9	7.524	-1.476	2.179	0.290
7	8.871	-1.871	3.501	0.395
40	36.594	3.406	11.601	0.317
9	10.535	-1.535	2.356	0.224
3	0.792	2.208	4.875	6.156
1	3.267	-2.267	5.139	1.573
1	0.941	0.059	0.001	0.001
			Total	9.024

Degree of Freedom = 4
Calculated X^2 value = 9.024
Table X^2 value at 5% level 9.448

Table 3.37 indicates that the calculated x^2 value is less than the table value at 5% level and hence the chi-square test reveals that the relationship between the social group of the employees and their attitude towards workers attitude is insignificant in Melur.

Null Hypothesis : Social Group of employees and their attitude towards workers attitude is independent in Andipatti.

TABLE 3.38

Social Group of Employees and their Attitude towards Workers Attitude - In Andipatti

x^2 - Test

O	E	O-E	$(O-E)^2$	$\dfrac{(O-E)^2}{E}$
4	2.423	1.573	2.474	1.021
2	6.462	-4.462	19.909	3.081
8	5.115	2.885	8.323	1.627
3	5.538	-2.538	6.441	1.163
19	14.770	4.230	17.893	1.211
10	11.692	-1.692	2.863	0.245
2	1.039	0.961	0.924	0.889
3	2.769	0.231	0.053	0.019
1	2.192	-1.192	1.421	0.648
			Total	9.904

Degree of Freedom   = 4

Calculated x^2 value   = 9.904

Table x^2 value at 5% level   9.448

      Table 3.38 indicates that the calculated x^2 value is higher than the table value at 5% level and hence the chi-square test reveals that the relationship between the social group of employees and their attitude towards workers attitude is significant in Andipatti.

Null Hypothesis : Social Group of employees and their
attitude towards job characteristics
is independent in Melur.

TABLE 3.39

Social Group of Employees and their Attitude towards
Job Characteristics - In Melur

$$x^2 - \text{Test}$$

O	E	O-E	$(O-E)^2$	$\dfrac{(O-E)^2}{E}$
6	4.119	1.881	3.538	0.859
14	16.990	-2.010	4.040	0.238
6	4.891	1.109	1.230	0.251
8	10.772	-2.772	7.683	0.713
49	44.436	4.564	20.830	0.469
11	12.792	0.208	0.043	0.001
2	1.109	0.891	0.794	0.716
3	4.574	-1.426	2.033	0.445
2	1.317	0.682	0.465	0.353
			Total	4.045

Degree of Freedom   = 4

Calculated x^2 value   = 4.045

Table x^2 value at 5% level   9.448

Table 3.39 indicates that the calculated X^2 value is less than the table value at 5% level and hence the chi-square test reveals that the relationship between the social group of the employees and their attitude towards job characteristics is insignificant in Melur.

Null Hypothesis : Social group of the employees and their attitude towards job characteristics is independent in Andipatti

TABLE 3.40

Social Group of Employees and their Attitude towards
Job Characteristics - In Andipatti
X^2 - Test

O	E	O-E	$(O-E)^2$	$\dfrac{(O-E)^2}{E}$
4	6.577 ○	-2.577	6.641	1.010
19	17.538	1.462	2.137	0.122
15	13.885	1.115	1.243	0.090
3	1.212	1.788	3.197	2.638
3	3.231	-0.231	0.053	0.017
1	2.557	-1.557	2.424	0.948
2	1.212	0.788	0.621	0.512
2	3.231	-1.231	1.515	0.469
3	2.557	0.443	0.196	0.077
			Total	5.883

Degree of Freedom   = 4

Calculated X^2 value   = 5.883

Table X^2 value at 5% level   9.448

Table 3.40 indicates that the calculated X^2 value is less than the table value at 5% level and hence the chi-square test reveals that the relationship between the social group of the employees and their attitude towards job characteristics is insignificant in Melur.

Null Hypothesis   :   Social group of employees and their
attitude towards working conditions
·is independent in Melur.

TABLE 3.41

Social Group of Employees and their Attitude towards
Working Conditions - In Melur
X^2 - Test

O	E	O-E	$(O-E)^2$	$\dfrac{(O-E)^2}{E}$
2	1.743	0.257	0.066	0.038
3	7.188	-4.188	17.539	2.440
6	2.069	3.931	15.453	7.469
3	9.505	-6.495	42.185	4.438
50	39.208	10.792	116.467	2.970
7	11.287	-4.287	18.378	1.628
11	4.752	6.248	39.638	8.215
13	19.604	-6.604	43.613	2.225
6	5.644	0.356	0.127	0.022
			Total	29.445

Degree of Freedom   ▬ 4

Calculated X^2 value   ▬ 29.445

Table X^2 value at 5% level   9.488

Table 3.41 indicates that the calculated X^2 value
is higher than the table value at 5% level and hence the chi-
square test reveals that the relationship between the social
group of employees and their attitude towards working conditions is significant in Melur.

Null Hypothesis : Social Group of employees and their
attitude towards working conditions
is independent in Andipatti.

TABLE 3.42

Social Group of Employees and their Attitude towards
Working Conditions - In Andipatti

X^2 - Test

O	E	O-E	$(O-E)^2$	$\frac{(O-E)^2}{E}$
1	0.519	0.481	0.231	0.446
1	1.385	-0.385	0.148	0.107
1	1.096	-0.096	0.001	0.001
3	4.327	-1.327	1.761	0.407
10	11.538	-1.538	2.365	0.205
12	9.135	2.865	8.208	0.899
5	4.154	0.846	0.716	0.172
13	11.077	1.923	3.698	0.334
6	8.769	-2.769	7.667	0.874
			Total	3.445

Degree of Freedom   =   4

Calculated X^2 value   =   3.445

Table X^2 value at 5% level   9.448

     Table 3.43 indicates that the calculated X^2 value is less than the table value at 5% level and hence the chi-square test reveals that the relationship between the social group of the employees and their attitude towards working conditions is insignificant in Andipatti.

Null Hypothesis : Social group of employees and their
attitude towards personnel policies
is independent in Melur.

TABLE 3.43

Social Group of Employees and their Attitude towards
Personnel Policies - In Melur
X^2 - Test

O	E	O-E	$(O-E)^2$	$\frac{(O-E)^2}{E}$
1	0.792	0.208	0.043	0.055
3	3.267	-0.267	0.071	0.022
1	0.941	0.059	0.001	0.001
3	6.653	-3.653	13.344	2.006
25	27.446	-2.446	5.983	0.213
14	7.901	6.091	37.100	4.696
12	8.555	3.445	11.868	1.387
38	35.287	2.713	7.360	0.209
4	10.158	-6.158	37.921	3.733
			Total	12.322

Degree of Freedom = 4
Calculated X^2 value = 12.322
Table X^2 value at 5% level 9.488

Table 3.43 indicates that the calculated X^2 value is higher than the table value at 5% level and hence the chi-square test reveals that the relationship between the social group of the employees and their attitude towards personnel policies is significant in Melur.

Null Hypothesis : Social group of employees and their attitude towards personnel policies is independent in Andipatti.

TABLE 3.44

Social Group of Employees and their Attitude towards Personnel Policies - In Andipatti

X^2 - Test

O	E	O-E	$(O-E)^2$	$\dfrac{(O-E)^2}{E}$
2	3.115	-1.115	1.243	0.399
11	8.308	2.692	7.247	0.872
5	6.577	-1.577	2.487	0.378
7	5.885	1.115	1.243	0.211
13	15.692	-2.692	7.247	0.462
14	12.423	1.577	2.487	0.200
			Total	2.522

Degree of Freedom   = 2

Calculated X^2 value   = 2.522

Table X^2 value at 5% level   5.991

Table 3.44 indicates that the calculated x^2 value is less than the table value at 5% level and hence the chi-square test reveals that the relationship between the social group of the employees and their attitude towards personnel policies is insignificant in Andipatti.

Null Hypothesis : Social group of employees and their attitude towards performance reward relationship is independent in Melur.

TABLE 3.45

Social Group of Employees and their Attitude towards Performance Reward Relationship-In Melur

x^2 - Test

O	E	O-E	$(O-E)^2$	$\dfrac{(O-E)^2}{E}$
0	0.476	-0.476	0.227	0.476
2	1.960	0.040	0.001	0.001
1	0.564	0.436	0.190	0.337
8	4.911	3.089	9.542	1.943
11	20.257	-9.257	85.692	4.230
12	5.832	6.168	88.044	0.523
8	10.614	-2.614	6.833	0.644
53	43.782	9.218	84.972	1.941
6	12.604	-6.604	43.613	3.460
			Total	19.555

Degree of Freedom $=$ 4

Calculated X^2 value $=$ 19.555

Table X^2 value at 5% level 9.488

Table 3.45 indicates that the calculated X^2 value is higher than the table value at 5% level and hence the chi-square test reveals that the relationship between the social group of the employees and their attitude towards performance reward relationship is significant in Melur.

Null Hypothesis :   Social group of employees and their
                     attitude performance reward relation-
                     ship is independent in Andipatti.

TABLE 3.46

Social Group of Employees and their Attitude towards
Performance Reward Relationship -
In Andipatti
X^2 - Test

O	E	O-E	$(O-E)^2$	$\frac{(O-E)^2}{E}$
1	0.173	0.827	0.684	3.953
0	0.462	-0.462	0.213	0.462
0	0.365	-0.365	0.133	0.365
5	2.596	2.404	5.779	2.226
7	6.923	0.077	0.001	0.001
3	5.481	-2.481	6.155	1.123
3	6.231	-3.231	10.439	1.675
17	16.615	0.385	0.148	0.001
16	13.154	2.846	8.010	0.616
			Total	10.422

Degree of Freedom   =   4

Calculated X^2 value   =   10.422

Table X^2 value at 5% level 9.488

Table 3.46 indicates that the calculated x^2 value is higher than the table value at 5% level and hence the chi-square test reveals that the relationship between the social group of the employees and their attitude towards performance reward relationship is significant in Andipatti.

Null Hypothesis : Social group of employees and their attitude towards supervision is independent in Melur

TABLE 3.47

Social Group of Employees and their Attitude towards Supervision - In Melur
x^2 - Test

O	E	O-E	$(O-E)^2$	$\dfrac{(O-E)^2}{E}$
3	2.535	0.465	0.216	0.085
9	10.455	-1.455	2.117	0.202
4	3.010	0.990	0.980	0.326
7	12.198	-5.198	27.019	2.215
56	50.317	5.683	32.296	0.642
14	14.485	-0.485	0.235	0.016
6	1.267	4.733	22.401	17.681
1	5.228	-4.228	17.876	3.419
1	1.505	-0.505	0.255	0.169
			Total	24.755

Degree of Freedom   =   4

Calculated x^2 value   =   24.755

Table x^2 value at 5% level   9.488

       Table 3.47 indicates that the calculated x^2 value is higher than the table value at 5% level and hence the chi-square test reveals that the relationship between the social group of the employees and their attitude towards supervision is significant in Melur.

Null Hypothesis : Social group of employees and their
attitude towards supervision is independent in Andipatti

TABLE 3.48

Social Group of Employees and their Attitude towards
Supervision - In Andipatti

x^2 - Test

O	E	O-E	$(O-E)^2$	$\dfrac{(O-E)^2}{E}$
2	0.865	1.135	1.288	1.489
2	2.308	-0.308	0.095	0.041
1	1.827	-0.827	0.684	0.374
5	6.404	-1.404	1.971	0.308
15	17.077	-2.077	4.314	0.253
17	13.519	3.481	12.117	0.896
2	1.731	0.269	0.072	0.042
7	4.615	2.385	5.688	1.233
1	3.654	-2.654	7.044	1.928
			Total	6.564

Degree of Freedom = 4

Calculated x^2 value = 6.564

Table x^2 value at 5% level   9.488

Table 3.48 indicates that the calculated x^2 value is less than the table value at 5% level and hence the chi-square test reveals that the relationship between the social group of the employees and their attitude towards supervision is insignificant in Andipatti.

Null Hypothesis : Social group of employees and their attitude towards communication is independent in Melur.

TABLE 3.49

Social Group of Employees and their Attitude towards Communication - In Melur

x^2 - Test

O	E	O-E	$(O-E)^2$	$\dfrac{(O-E)^2}{E}$
6	2.376	3.624	13.133	5.528
2	9.802	-7.802	60.871	6.210
7	2.822	4.178	17.456	6.186
5	11.564	-6.564	43.086	3.726
59	47.703	7.297	53.246	1.116
9	13.733	-4.733	22.401	1.631
5	2.059	2.941	8.649	4.201
5	8.495	-3.495	12.215	1.438
3	2.446	0.554	0.307	0.125
			Total	30.161

Degree of Freedom $\quad$ = $\quad$ 4

Calculated X^2 value $\quad$ = $\quad$ 30.161

Table X^2 value at 5% level $\quad$ = $\quad$ 9.488

$\quad$ Table 3.49 indicates that the calculated X^2 value is higher than the table value at 5% level and hence the chi-square test reveals that the relationship between the social group of the employees and their attitude towards communication is significant in Melur.

Null Hypothesis : Social group of employees and their

attitude towards communication is

independent in Andipatti.

TABLE 3.50

Social Group of Employees and their Attitude towards
Communication - In Andipatti
x^2 - Test

O	E	O-E	$(O-E)^2$	$\frac{(O-E)^2}{E}$
1	0.346	0.654	0.428	1.236
1	0.923	0.077	0.001	0.001
0	0.731	-0.731	0.534	0.731
4	3.462	0.538	0.289	0.084
8	9.231	-1.231	1.515	0.164
8	7.307	0.693	0.480	0.065
4	5.192	-1.192	1.421	0.274
15	13.846	2.154	6.320	0.456
11	10.962	0.038	0.001	0.001
			Total	3.012

Degree of Freedom = 4

Calculated x^2 value = 3.012

Table x^2 value at 5% level 9.488

Table 3.50 indicates that the calculated X^2 value
is less than the table value at 5% level and hence the chi-
square test reveals that the relationship between the social
group of the employees and their attitude towards communication is insignificant in Andipatti.

Null Hypothesis : Social Group of employees and their
attitude towards Organization Climate
is independent in Melur.

.TABLE 3.51

Social Group of Employees and their Attitude towards
Organizational Climate - In Melur
X^2 - Test

O	E	O-E	$(O-E)^2$	$\dfrac{(O-E)^2}{E}$
3	1.901	1.099	1.208	0.635
10	12.515	-2.515	6.325	0.505
3	1.584	1.416	2.005	1.266
7	7.842	-0.842	0.709	0.090
57	51.624	5.376	28.901	0.560
2	6.535	-4.535	20.566	3.147
2	2.257	-0.257	0.066	0.029
12	14.861	-2.861	8.185	0.551
5	1.881	3.119	9.728	5.172
			Total	12.765

Degree of Freedom   = 4

Calculated x^2 value   = 12.765

Table x^2 value at 5% level 9.488

      Table 3.51 indicates that the calculated x^2 value is higher than the table value at 5% level and hence the chi-square test reveals that the relationship between the social group of the employees and their attitude towards Organizatio Climate is significant in Melur.

Null Hypothesis : Social Group of employees and their

attitude towards Organizational

Climate is independent in Andipatti

TABLE 3.52

Social Group of Employees and their Attitude towards
Organizational Climate - In Andipatti
X^2 - Test

O	E	O-E	$(O-E)^2$	$\dfrac{(O-E)^2}{E}$
2	1.558	0.442	0.195	0.125
5	5.712	-0.712	0.507	0.089
2	1.730	0.270	0.073	0.042
3	4.154	-1.154	1.332	0.321
18	15.231	2.769	7.667	0.503
3	4.615	-1.615	2.608	0.565
4	3.288	0.712	0.507	0.154
10	12.058	-2.058	4.235	0.351
5	3.654	1.346	1.812	0.496
			Total	2.646

Degree of Freedom   = 4

Calculated X^2 value   = 2.646

Table X^2 value at 5% level 9.488

Table 3.52 indicates that the calculated x^2 value is less than the table value at 5% level and hence the chi-square test reveals that the relationship between the social group of the employees and their attitude towards Organizational Climate is insignificant in Andipatti.

From the above tests the following conclusions have been drawn.

In Melur the social group of the employees and their attitude towards workers attitude, job characteristics have insignificant relationship and working conditions. Personnel policies, performance reward relationship, supervision and communication have significant relationship.

In Andipatti, the social group of the employees and their attitude towards workers attitude performance reward relationship have significant relationship and other dimensions viz. Job characteristics, personnel policies, supervision and communications have insignificant relationship with the attitudes of employees in Andipatti.

The relationship the social group of the employees and their attitude towards Organizational Climate is significant in Melur and insignificant in Andipatti. Hence the hypothesis the social group of the employees has influence

over their attitude towards Organizational Climate has been
accepted in Melur and rejected in Andipatti.

3.5   CONCLUSION

In this chapter, the Personal Factors influencing
the attitude of the employees have been analysed by using the
chi-square test.   To analyse the personal factors influencing the Organizational Climate, the following hypotheses
have been framed.

1) The age of the employees influences their
attitude towards Organizational Climate.

2) The education of the employees influences
their attitude towards Organizational
Climate.

3) The social group of the employees influences
their attitude towards Organizational Climate.

The analysis reveals that, age, education and
social group have influence over the employee's attitude
towards Organizational Climate in Melur unit.

In Andipatti, the analysis reveals that age has influence over the employee's attitude towards Organizational Climate. Education and social group of the employees have no impact on their attitude towards Organizational Climate.

CHAPTER IV

EMPLOYEES ATTITUDE TOWARDS ORGANIATIONAL

CLIMATE PERTAINING TO JOB FACTORS

4.1   INTRODUCTION

The attitude of the workers towards the different
dimensions of Organizational Climate in selected units have
been presented in this chapter.   Job factors influencing
the Organizational Climate have been analysed.   The primary
data collected from the respondents have been used to measure
the attitude of the workers and the job factors influencing
the different organizational dimensions.   The scoring scheme
has been presented in the previous chapter.

4.2   FACTORS INFLUENCING THE ORGANIZATIONAL CLIMATE

In order to study the job factors influencing the
Organizational Climate, the following hypotheses have been
framed.

1.   The level of management of the employee has influence
     over Organizational Climate.

2.   The work experience of the employee has association with
     Organizational Climate.

3.   The income of the employee influences the attitude of
     employees towards Organizational Climate.

In order to verify the hypotheses, all the seven dimensions are analysed separately.

4.2.1   Level of Management of the Employees has Influence over Organizational Climate:

TABLE 4.1

Level of Management of the Employees and
their Average Mean Score

Level of Management of Employees	Melur		Andipatti	
	Number of Employees	Average Mean Score	Number of Employees	Average Mean Score
Top	2	164.361	2	171.285
Middle	18	136.493	9	130.464
Low	81	143.896	41	127.827
Total	101		52	

Table 4.1 shows that, in both Melur and Andipatti units the employees who belong to top management have more favourable attitude towards Organizational Climate. Middle level management and low level management have less level of favourable towards Organizational Climate.

To test the correlation between the level of
management and its attitude towards Organizational Climate
chi-square test has been applied to all the dimensions of
Organizational Climate.

Null Hypothesis :   Level of management of employees and
                     its attitude towards workers attitude
                     is independent in Melur.

TABLE 4.2

Level of Management of Employees and its
Attitude towards Workers Atti-
tude - In Melur
X^2 - Test

O	E	O-E	$(O-E)^2$	$\dfrac{(O-E)^2}{E}$
2	0.792	1.208	1.459	1.848
11	7.129	3.871	14.985	2.102
27	32.079	4.921	24.216	0.755
0	1.109	-1.109	1.203	1.109
5	9.980	-4.980	24.800	2.485
50	44.911	5.089	25.895	0.577
0	0.099	-0.099	0.001	0.099
2	0.891	1.109	1.230	1.380
			Total	10.355

Degree of Freedom   = 4

Calculated X^2 value   = 10.355

Table X^2 value at 5% level 9.488

Table 4.2 indicates that the calculated X^2 value is higher than the table value at 5% level and hence the chi-square test reveals that the relationship between the level of management of employees and its attitude towards workers attitude is significant in Melur.

Null Hypothesis : Level of Management of employees and its
attitude towards workers attitude is
independent in Andipatti.

TABLE 4.3

Level of Management of Employees and its Attitude
towards Workers Attitude-In Andipatti
X^2 - Test

O	E	O-E	$(O-E)^2$	$\dfrac{(O-E)^2}{E}$
1	0.539	0.461	0.213	0.394
5	2.423	2.577	6.641	2.741
8	11.038	-3.038	9.229	0.836
1	1.231	-0.231	0.053	0.043
3	5.538	-2.538	6.441	1.163
28	25.231	2.769	7.667	0.304
0	0.231	-0.231	0.053	0.231
1	1.038	-0.038	0.001	0.001
5	4.731	0.269	0.072	0.015
			Total	5.728

Degree of Freedom = 4

Calculated X^2 value = 5.728

Table X^2 value at 5% level of 9.488

Table 4.3 indicates that the calculated x^2 value is less than the Table x^2 value at 5% level and hence the chi-square test reveals that the relationship between the level of management of employees and its attitude towards workers attitude is insignificant in Andipatti.

Null Hypothesis : Level of Management of employees and its attitude towards job characteristics is independent in Melur.

TABLE 4.4

Level of Management of Employees and its Attitude towards Job Characteristics - In Melur
x^2 - Test

O	E	O-E	$(O-E)^2$	$\dfrac{(O-E)^2}{E}$
2	0.515	1.485	2.205	4.282
9	4.684	4.366	19.062	4.113
15	20.815	-5.851	34.234	1.642
0	1.347	-1.347	1.814	1.347
7	12.119	-5.119	26.204	2.162
61	54.534	6.466	41.809	0.767
0	0.139	-0.139	0.019	0.139
2	1.247	0.753	0.567	0.455
5	5.614	-0.614	0.377	0.067
			Total	14.974

Degree of Freedom = 4

Calculated X^2 value = 14.974

Table X^2 value at 5% level 9.488

Table 4.4 indicates that the calculated X^2 value is higher than the table value at 5% level and hence the chi-square test reveals that the relationship between the level of management of employees and its attitude towards job characteristics is significant in Melur.

Null Hypothesis : Level of management of employees and its attitude towards job characteristics is independent in Andipatti.

TABLE 4.5

Level of Management of Employees and its Attitude towards Job Characteristics - In Andipatti

x^2 - Test

O	E	O-E	$(O-E)^2$	$\frac{(O-E)^2}{E}$
2	1.462	0.538	0.289	0.198
7	6.577	0.423	0.179	0.027
29	29.961	-0.961	0.924	0.031
0	0.269	-0.269	0.072	0.269
1	1.212	-0.212	0.045	0.037
6	5.519	0.481	0.231	0.042
0	0.269	-0.269	0.072	0.269
1	1.212	-0.212	0.045	0.037
6	5.519	0.481	0.231	0.042
			Total	0.952

Degree of Freedom = 4

Calculated x^2 value = 0.952

Table x^2 value at 5% level 0.952

Table 4.5 indicates that the calculated x^2 value
is less than the table value at 5% level and hence the chi-
square test reveals that the relationship between the level
of management of employees and its attitude towards job
characteristics is significant in Andipatti.

Null Hypothesis : Level of management of employees and its
attitude towards working conditions is
independent in Melur

TABLE 4.6

Level of Management of Employees and its Attitude
towards Working Conditions - In Melur

x^2 - Test

O	E	O-E	$(O-E)^2$	$\frac{(O-E)^2}{E}$
0	0.218	-0.218	0.048	0.218
1	1.960	-0.960	0.922	0.470
10	8.822	1.178	1.388	0.157
1	1.188	-0.188	0.035	0.030
6	10.693	-4.693	22.024	2.060
53	48.119	4.881	23.824	0.495
1	0.594	0.406	0.165	0.278
11	5.347	5.653	31.956	5.977
18	24.059	-6.059	36.711	1.526
			Total	11.211

Degree of Freedom   = 4

Calculated x^2 value   = 11.211

Table x^2 value at 5% level   9.488

Table 4.6 indicates that the calculated x^2 value is higher than the table value at 5% level and hence chi-square test reveals that the relationship between the level of management of employees and its attitude towards working conditions is significant in Melur.

Null Hypothesis : Level of Management of employees and its
attitude towards working conditions is
independent in Andipatti.

TABLE 4.7

Level of Management of Employees and its Attitude towards
Working Conditions - In Andipatti
X^2 - Test

O	E	O-E	$(O-E)^2$	$\dfrac{(O-E)^2}{E}$
1	0.115	0.885	0.783	6.811
1	0.520	0.480	0.230	0.443
1	2.365	-1.365	1.863	0.788
1	0.962	0.083	0.001	0.001
6	4.327	1.673	2.799	0.661
18	19.711	-1.711	2.928	0.149
0	0.923	-0.923	0.852	0.903
2	4.154	-2.154	6.320	1.521
22	18.923	3.077	9.468	0.500
			Total	11.777

Degree of Freedom   = 4

Calculated X^2 value   = 11.777

Table X^2 value at 5% level 9.488

Table 4.7 indicates that the calculated x^2 value is higher than the table value and hence the chi-square test reveals that the relationship between the level of management of the employees and its attitude towards working conditions is significant in Andipatti.

Null Hypothesis : Level of Management of employees and its
attitude towards personnel policies is
independent in Melur.

TABLE 4.8

Level of Management of Employees and its Attitude towards
Personnel Policies - In Melur
x^2 - Test

O	E	O-E	$(O-E)^2$	$\frac{(O-E)^2}{E}$
1	0.099	0.901	0.812	8.200
2	0.891	1.109	1.230	1.380
2	4.010	-2.010	4.040	1.008
1	0.832	0.168	0.028	0.034
7	7.485	-0.485	0.235	0.037
34	33.683	0.317	0.100	0.001
0	1.069	-1.069	1.143	1.069
9	9.624	-0.624	6.389	0.040
45	43.307	1.693	2.866	0.066
			Total	11.835

Degree of Freedom   = 4

Calculated x^2 value   = 11.835

Table x^2 value at 5% level = 9.488

      Table 4.8 indicates that the calculated x^2 value is higher than the table value and hence the chi-square test reveals that the relationship between the level of management of the employee and its attitude towards personnel policies is significant in Melur.

Null Hypothesis :   Level of management of employees and
                    its attitude towards personnel policies
                    is independent in Andipatti.

TABLE 4.9

Level of Management of Employees and its Attitude
towards Personnel Policies - In
Andipatti
x^2 - Test

O	E	O-E	$(O-E)^2$	$\dfrac{(O-E)^2}{E}$
1	0.692	0.308	0.095	0.137
8	3.115	4.885	23.863	7.661
9	14.193	-5.193	26.967	1.900
1	1.308	-0.308	0.095	0.073
1	5.885	-4.885	23.863	4.055
32	26.807	5.193	26.967	1.006
			Total	14.832

Degree of Freedom   = 2

Calculated x^2 value   = 14.832

Table x^2 value at 5% level 5.991

Table 4.9 indicates that the calculated x^2 value
is higher than the table value at 5% level and hence the

chi-square test reveals that the relationship between the
level of management of employees and its attitude towards
personnel policies is significant in Andipatti.

Null Hypothesis : Level of management of employees and
its attitude towards performance
reward relationship is independent in
Melur

TABLE 4.10

Level of Management of Employees and its Attitude
towards Performance Reward Relation-
ship - In Melur

X^2 - Test

O	E	O-E	$(O-E)^2$	$\frac{(O-E)^2}{E}$
0	0.059	-0.059	0.001	0.059
1	0.535	0.465	0.216	0.404
2	2.406	-0.406	0.165	0.069
1	0.614	0.386	0.149	0.243
12	5.525	6.475	41.926	7.588
18	24.861	-6.861	47.073	1.893
1	1.327	-0.327	0.107	0.081
5	11.941	-6.941	48.177	4.035
61	53.732	7.268	52.824	0.983
			Total	15.355

Degree of Freedom   =   4

Calculated x^2 value   =   15.355

Table x^2 value at 5% level   9.488

       Table 4.10 indicates that the calculated x^2 value is higher than the table value and hence the chi-square test reveals that the relationship between the level of management of the employees and their attitude towards performance reward relationship is significant in Melur.

Null Hypothesis : Level of management of employees and
its attitude towards performance reward
relationship is independent in Andipatti

TABLE 4.11

Level of Management of Employees and its Attitude
towards Performance Reward Relation-
ship - In Andipatti

x^2 - Test

O	E	O-E	$(O-E)^2$	$\dfrac{(O-E)^2}{E}$
0	0.038	0.038	0.001	0.038
0	0.173	0.173	0.029	0.173
1	0.789	0.211	0.045	0.056
2	0.577	1.423	2.025	3.509
5	2.596	2.404	5.779	2.262
8	11.827	-3.827	14.646	1.238
0	1.385	-1.385	1.918	1.385
4	6.231	-2.231	4.977	0.799
32	28.384	3.616	13.075	0.461
			Total	9.921

Degree of Freedom   = 4

Calculated x^2 value   = 9.921

Table x^2 value at 5% level 9.488

Table 4.11 indicates that the calculated x^2 value is higher than the table value at 5% level and hence the chi-square test reveals that the relationship between the level of management of the employees and its attitude towards performance reward relationship is significant in Andipatti.

Null Hypothesis : Level of management of employees and its attitude towards supervision is independent in Melur.

TABLE 4.12

Level of Management of Employees and its Attitude towards Supervision - In Melur
x^2 - Test

O	E	O-E	$(O-E)^2$	$\dfrac{(O-E)^2}{E}$
2	0.317	1.683	2.832	8.934
8	2.851	5.149	26.512	9.299
6	12.832	-6.832	46.676	3.637
0	1.525	-1.525	2.326	1.525
7	13.723	-6.723	45.199	3.294
70	61.752	8.248	68.029	1.102
0	0.158	-0.158	0.025	0.158
3	1.426	1.574	2.477	1.737
5	6.416	-1.416	2.005	0.312
			Total	29.998

Degree of Freedom   =   4

Calculated x^2 value   =   29.998

Table x^2 value at 5% level   9.448

       Table 4.12 indicates that the calculated x^2 value is higher than the table value at 5% level and hence the chi-square test reveals that the relationship between the level of management of the employees and its attitude towards supervision is significant in Melur.

Null Hypothesis : Level of management of employees and
its attitude towards supervision is
independent in Andipatti.

TABLE 4.13

Level of Management of Employees and its
Attitude towards Supervision -
In Andipatti
x^2 - Test

O	E	O-E	$(O-E)^2$	$\dfrac{(O-E)^2}{E}$
1	0.192	0.808	0.653	3.400
0	0.866	-0.866	0.750	0.866
4	3.942	0.058	0.001	0.001
1	1.423	-0.423	0.179	0.126
6	6.404	-0.404	0.163	0.025
30	29.173	0.827	0.683	0.023
0	0.385	0.385	0.148	0.385
3	1.730	1.270	1.613	0.032
7	7.885	-0.885	0.783	0.099
			Total	5.857

Degree of Freedom   = 4

Calculated x^2 value   = 5.857

Table x^2 value at 5% level 9.488

Table 4.13 indicates that the calculated X^2 value is less than the table value at 5% level and hence the chi-square test reveals that the relationship between the level of management of the employees and its attitude towards supervision is insignificant in Andipatti.

Null Hypothesis : Level of management of employees and its attitude towards communication is independent in Melur

TABLE 4.14

Level of Management of Employees and its
towards Communication - In
Melur

X^2 - Test

O	E	O-E	$(O-E)^2$	$\frac{(O-E)^2}{E}$
2	0.297	1.703	2.900	9.765
9	2.673	6.327	40.031	14.976
4	12.030	-8.030	64.481	5.360
0	1.446	-1.446	2.091	1.446
4	13.010	-9.010	81.180	6.240
69	58.544	8.456	89.416	1.527
0	0.257	-0.257	0.060	0.257
5	2.317	2.683	7.198	3.107
8	10.426	-2.426	5.885	0.564
				Total 43.242

Degree of Freedom   = 4

Calculated X^2 value   = 43.242

Table X^2 value at 5% level   9.488

      Table 4.14 indicates that the calculated X^2 value is higher than the table value at 5% level and hence the chi-square test reveals that the relationship between the level of management of the employees and its attitude towards communication is significant in Melur.

Null Hypothesis : Level of management of employees and its attitude towards communication is independent in Andipatti.

TABLE 4.15

Level of Management of Employees and its
Attitude towards Communication-
In Andipatti
x^2 - Test

O	E	O-E	$(O-E)^2$	$\dfrac{(O-E)^2}{E}$
2	0.077	1.921	3.690	47.925
0	0.346	-0.346	0.120	0.346
0	1.577	-1.577	2.487	1.577
0	1.154	-1.154	1.332	1.154
7	5.192	1.808	3.267	0.630
23	23.654	-0.654	0.428	0.018
0	0.769	-0.769	0.591	0.769
2	3.462	-1.462	2.137	0.617
18	15.769	2.231	4.977	0.316
			Total	53.352

Degree of Freedom   =   4

Calculated x^2 value   =   53.352

Table x^2 value at 5% level   9.488

Table 4.15 indicates that the calculated x^2
value is higher than the table value at 5% level and hence
the chi-square test reveals that the relationship between
the level of management of the employees and its attitude
towards communication is significant in Andipatti.

Null Hypothesis : Level of management of employees and its
attitude towards Organizational Climate
is independent in Melur.

TABLE 4.16

Level of Management of Employees and its Attitude
towards Organizational Climate - In
Melur
x^2 - Test

O	E	O-E	$(O-E)^2$	$\frac{(O-E)^2}{E}$
1	0.238	0.762	0.581	2.441
4	2.139	1.861	3.463	1.619
7	9.623	-2.623	5.121	1.879
1	1.504	-0.564	0.318	0.203
6	14.080	-8.080	65.286	4.637
72	63.356	8.644	74.719	1.179
0	0.198	-0.198	0.039	0.197
8	1.782	6.218	38.663	21.696
2	8.020	-6.020	36.240	4.519
			Total	38.370

Degree of Freedom   = 4

Calculated X^2 value   = 38.370

Table X^2 value at 5% level 9.488

Table 4.16 indicates that the calculated X^2 value is higher than the table value at 5% level and hence the chi-square test reveals that the relationship between the level of management of employees and its attitude towards Organizational Climate is significant in Melur.

Null Hypothesis : Level of Management of employees and
its attitude towards Organizational
Climate is independent in Andipatti.

TABLE 4.17

Level of Management of Employees and its Attitude
towards Organizational Climate -
In Andipatti
x^2 - Test

O	E	O-E	$(O-E)^2$	$\frac{(O-E)^2}{E}$
1	0.346	0.654	0.428	1.237
4	1.558	2.442	5.963	3.828
4	7.096	-3.096	9.585	1.351
1	1.269	-0.269	0.072	0.057
1	5.712	-4.712	22.203	3.887
31	26.019	4.981	24.810	0.954
0	0.385	-0.385	0.148	0.385
4	1.731	2.269	5.149	2.975
6	7.884	-1.884	3.549	0.450
			Total	15.124

Degree of Freedom = 4

Calculated x^2 value = 15.124

Table x^2 value at 5% level 9.488

Table 4.17 indicates that the calculated x^2 value is higher than the table value at 5% level and hence the chi-square test reveals that the relationship between the level of management of employees and its attitude towards Organizational Climate is significant in Andipatti.

The following conclusions have been drawn from the above tests.

The level of management of the employee and its attitude towards all the dimensions viz, workers attitude, job characteristics, working conditions personnel policies, performance reward relationship, supervision, and communication have significant relationship in Melur.

The level of management of the employee and its attitude towards workers attitude, job characteristics, supervision have insignificant relationship in Andipatti and working conditions, personnel policy, performance reward relationship, and communication have significant relationship in Andipatti.

The level of management of the employee and its attitude towards Organizational Climate is significant in both Melur and Andipatti. Hence the hypothesis the level of management of the employee influences the Organizational Climate has been accepted in both Melur and Andipatti.

4.2.2   Work Experience of the Employee has Association
        with Organizational Climate

TABLE 4.18

Work Experience of Employees and their
Average Mean Score

Work Experience of Employees	Melur		Andipatti	
	Number of Employees	Average Mean Score	Number of Employees	Average Mean Score
Below 3 years	-	-	7	156.346
3-5 years	-	-	14	149.642
More than 5 years	-	-	31	123.588
Below 10 years	13	149.724	-	-
10-20 years	44	119.846	-	-
211 and above	44	175.180	-	-
Total	101		52	

       Table 4.18 shows that, work experience is different
in two units. Melur mill has more experienced workers than
Andipatti mill.   So, two different classifications have been
made to test the relationship between work experience of the
employees and their attitude towards Organizational Climate.

In Melur mill, experienced employees consider
Organizational Climate to be good. Contradictory to this,
in Andipatti mill experienced employees consider that the
Organizational Climate is not good. To test the relationship between the work experience of the workers and their
attitude towards Organizational Climate chi-square test has
been applied.

Null Hypothesis : Work experience of employees and their
attitude towards workers attitude is
independent in Melur.

TABLE 4.19

Work Experience of Employees and their Attitude
towards Workers Attitude-In Melur

$$x^2 - \text{Test}$$

O	E	O-E	$(O-E)^2$	$\dfrac{(O-E)^2}{E}$
8	5.149	2.851	8.128	1.579
19	17.425	1.575	2.471	0.142
13	17.426	-4.426	19.589	1.124
2	7.208	-5.208	27.124	3.763
24	24.396	-0.396	0.157	0.001
30	24.396	5.604	31.405	1.287
3	0.644	2.356	5.551	8.619
1	2.178	-1.178	13.877	0.637
1	2.178	-1.178	13.877	0.637
			Total	17.789

Degree of Freedom   =   4

Calculated x^2 value   =   17.789

Table x^2 value at 5% level   9.488

        Table 4.19 indicates that the calculated x^2 value is higher than the table value at 5% level and hence the chi-square test reveals that the relationship between the work experience of the employee and their attitude towards workers attitude is significant in Melur.

Null Hypothesis : Work experience of employees and their

attitude towards workers attitude is

independent in Andipatti.

TABLE 4.20

Work Experience of Employees and their Attitude
towards Workers Attitude - In
Andipatti
x^2 - Test

O	E	O-E	$(O-E)^2$	$\dfrac{(O-E)^2}{E}$
1	1.885	-0.885	0.783	0.416
6	3.769	2.231	4.977	1.321
7	8.346	-1.346	1.812	0.217
4	4.308	-0.308	0.095	0.022
6	8.614	-2.614	6.833	0.793
22	19.076	1.924	3.702	0.194
2	0.808	1.192	1.421	1.758
2	1.615	0.385	0.148	0.092
2	3.577	-1.577	2.487	0.695
			Total	5.508

Degree of Freedom   = 4

Calculated x^2 value   = 5.508

Table x^2 value at 5% level   9.488

Table 4.20 indicates that the calculated x^2 value is less than the table value at 5% level and hence the chi-square test reveals that the relationship between the work experience of employees and their attitude towards workers attitude is insignificant in Andipatti.

Null Hypothesis : Work experience of employees and their attitude towards job characteristics is independent in Melur.

TABLE 4.21

Work Experience of Employees and their Attitude towards Job Characteristics - In Melur

x^2 - Test

O	E	O-E	$(O-E)^2$	$\frac{(O-E)^2}{E}$
7	3.347	3.653	13.344	3.987
10	11.326	-1.326	1.758	0.155
9	11.327	-2.327	5.415	0.478
4	8.752	-4.752	22.582	2.580
32	29.624	2.376	5.645	0.191
32	29.624	9.376	5.645	0.191
2	0.901	1.099	1.208	1.341
2	3.050	-1.050	1.216	0.398
2	3.049	-0.049	0.001	0.001
			Total	9.322

Degree of Freedom   =   4

Calculated x^2 value   =   9.322

Table x^2 value at 5% level   9.488

      -Table 4.21 indicates that the calculated x^2 is less than the table value at 5% level of significant and hence the chi-square table reveals that the relationship between the work experience of employees and their attitude towards job characteristics in Melur is insignificant.

Null Hypothesis : Work experience of employees and their attitude towards job characteristics is independent in Andipatti.

TABLE 4.22

Work Experience of Employees and their Attitude towards Job Characteristics - In Andipatti

x^2 - Test

O	E	O-E	$(O-E)^2$	$\left(\dfrac{O-E}{E}\right)^2$
3	5.115	-2.115	4.473	0.875
10	10.232	-0.232	0.054	0.001
25	22.653	2.347	5.508	0.243
3	0.942	2.058	4.235	4.496
4	1.885	2.115	4.473	2.373
0	4.173	-4.173	17.414	4.173
1	0.942	0.058	0.001	0.001
0	1.885	-1.885	3.553	1.885
6	4.173	1.827	3.338	0.800
			Total	14.847

Degree of Freedom   = 4

Calculated x^2 value   = 14.847

Table x^2 value at 5% level 9.488

Table 4.22 indicates that the calculated x^2
value is higher than the table value at 5% level and hence
the chi-square test reveals that the relationship between
the work experience of employees and their attitude towards
job characteristics is significant in Andipatti.

Null Hypothesis   :   Work experience of employees and their
                        attitude towards working conditions
                        is independent in Melur.

TABLE 4.23

Work Experience of Employees and their Attitude
towards Working Conditions - In
Melur

x^2 - Test

O	E	O-E	$(O-E)^2$	$\frac{(O-E)^2}{E}$
1	1.416	-0.416	0.173	0.122
8	4.792	3.208	10.291	2.148
2	4.792	-2.792	7.795	1.627
7	7.723	-0.723	0.523	0.068
23	26.138	-3.138	9.847	0.377
30	26.139	3.861	14.907	0.370
5	3.862	1.138	1.295	0.335
13	13.069	-0.069	0.001	0.001
12	13.069	-1.069	1.143	0.087
			Total	5.335

Degree of Freedom   =   4

Calculated X^2 value   =   5.335

Table X^2 value at 5% level   9.488

      Table 4.23 indicates that the calculated X^2 value is less than the table value at 5% level and hence the chi-square test reveals that the relationship between the work experience of employees and their attitude towards working conditions is insignificant in Melur.

Null Hypothesis : Work experience of employees and their attitude towards working conditions is independent in Andipatti.

TABLE 4.24

Work Experience of Employees and their Attitude
towards Working Conditions - In
Andipatti
X^2 - Test

O	E	O-E	$(O-E)^2$	$\frac{(O-E)^2}{E}$
1	0.404	0.596	0.355	0.879
0	0.808	-0.808	0.653	0.808
2	1.788	0.212	0.045	0.025
4	3.365	0.635	0.403	0.120
3	6.731	-3.731	13.920	2.068
18	14.904	3.096	9.585	0.643
2	3.231	-1.231	1.515	0.469
11	6.462	4.538	20.593	3.187
11	14.307	-3.307	10.936	0.764
			Total	8.963

Degree of Freedom   =   4

Calculated X^2 value   =   8.963

Table X^2 value at 5% level   9.488

Table 4.24 indicates that the calculated X^2 value is less than the table value at 5% level and hence the chi-square test reveals that the relationship between the work experience of employees and their attitude towards working conditions is insignificant in Andipatti.

Null Hypothesis : Work experience of employees and their attitude towards personnel policies is independent in Melur

TABLE 4.25

Work Experience of Employees and their Attitude
towards Personnel Policies - In
Melur

X^2 - Test

O	E	O-E	$(O-E)^2$	$\frac{(O-E)^2}{E}$
3	0.644	2.356	5.551	8.619
1	2.178	-1.178	1.388	0.637
1	2.178	-1.178	1.388	0.637
3	5.406	-2.406	5.789	1.071
19	18.297	0.703	0.494	0.027
20	18.297	1.703	2.900	0.158
7	6.950	0.050	0.001	0.001
24	23.525	0.475	0.226	0.001
23	23.525	-0.525	0.276	0.012
			Total	11.163

Degree of Freedom   =   4

Calculated x^2 value   =   11.163

Table x^2 value at 5% level   =   9.448

        Table 4.25 indicates that the calculated x^2 value
is high than the table value at 5% level hence the chi-square
test indicates that the relationship between the work
experience of employees and their attitude towards personnel
policies is significant in Melur.

Null Hypothesis :   Work experience of employees and their

                      attitude towards personnel policies is

                      independent in Andipatti.

TABLE 4.26

Work Experience of Employees and their Attitude towards
Personnel Policies - In Andipatti

x^2 - Test

0	E	O-E	$(O-E)^2$	$\dfrac{(O-E)^2}{E}$
2	2.423	-0.423	0.179	0.074
7	4.846	2.154	4.640	0.957
9	10.731	-1.731	2.996	0.279
5	4.577	0.423	0.179	0.039
7	9.154	-2.154	4.640	0.507
22	20.269	1.731	2.996	0.148
			Total	2.004

Degree of Freedom   =   2

Calculated X^2 value   =   2.004

Table X^2 value at 5% level   5.991

       Table 4.26 indicates that the calculated X^2 value is less than the table X^2 value is at 5% level and hence the chi-square test reveals that the relationship between the work experience of employees and their attitude towards personnel policy is insignificant in Andipatti.

Null Hypothesis : Work experience of employees and their
attitude towards performance reward
relationship is independent in Melur

TABLE 4.27

Work Experience of Employees and their Attitude
towards Performance Reward Relationship - In Melur
X^2 - Test

O	E	O-E	$(O-E)^2$	$\frac{(O-E)^2}{E}$
0	0.386	-0.386	0.149	0.386
1	1.307	-0.307	0.094	0.072
2	1.307	0.693	0.480	0.367
4	3.990	0.010	0.001	0.001
21	13.505	7.495	56.175	4.160
6	13.505	-7.505	56.325	4.171
9	8.624	0.376	0.141	0.016
22	29.188	-7.188	51.667	1.770
36	29.188	6.812	46.403	1.590
			Total	12.533

Degree of Freedom = 4

Calculated X^2 value = 12.533

Table X^2 value at 5% level 9.488

Table 4.27 indicates that the calculated X^2 value is high than the table value at 5% level and hence the chi-square test reveals that the relationship between the work experience of employees and their attitude towards performance reward relationship is significant in Melur.

Null Hypothesis : Work experience of employees and their attitude towards performance reward relationship is independent in Andipatti

TABLE 4.28

Work Experience of Employees and their Attitude towards Performance Reward Relation- ship - In Andipatti

X^2 - Test

O	E	O-E	$(O-E)^2$	$\dfrac{(O-E)^2}{E}$
0	0.135	-0.135	0.018	0.135
1	0.269	0.731	0.534	1.986
0	0.596	-0.596	0.355	0.596
1	2.020	-1.020	1.040	0.515
10	4.088	5.960	35.545	8.803
4	8.942	-4.942	0.553	0.062
6	4.846	1.154	1.332	0.275
3	9.692	-6.692	44.782	4.621
27	21.462	5.538	30.669	1.429
			Total	18.422

Degree of Freedom   =   4

Calculated x^2 value   =   18.422

Table x^2 value at 5% level   9.488

        Table 4.28 indicates that the calculated x^2 value is high than the table x^2 value at 5% level and hence the chi-square test reveals that the work experience of employees and their attitude towards performance reward relationship is significant in Andipatti.

Null Hypothesis : Work experience of employees and their
attitude towards supervision is inde-
pendent in Melur.

TABLE 4.29

Work Experience of Employees and their Attitude
Towards Supervision-In Melur
x^2 - Test

O	E	O-E	$(O-E)^2$	$\dfrac{(O-E)^2}{E}$
6	2.060	3.940	15.524	7.536
2	6.970	-4.970	24.701	3.544
8	6.970	1.030	1.061	0.152
7	9.911	-2.911	8.474	0.855
39	33.544	5.456	29.768	0.887
31	33.545	-2.545	6.477	0.193
0	1.030	-1.030	1.061	1.030
3	3.485	-0.485	0.235	0.067
5	3.485	1.515	2.295	0.659
			Total	14.923

Degree of Freedom   = 4

Calculated x^2 value   = 14.923

Table x^2 value at 5% level   9.488

Table 4.29 indicates that the calculated x^2
value is high than the table value at 5% level and hence
the chi-square test reveals that the relationship between
the work experience of employees and their attitude towards
supervision is significant in Melur.

Null Hypothesis : Work experience of employees and their
attitude towards supervision is inde-
pendent in Andipatti.

TABLE 4.30

Work Experience of Employees and their Attitude
towards Supervision - In Andipatti
x^2 - Test

O	E	O-E	$(O-E)^2$	$\dfrac{(O-E)^2}{E}$
2	0.673	1.327	1.761	2.617
1	1.346	-0.346	0.120	0.089
2	2.981	-0.981	0.962	0.323
2	4.981	-2.981	8.886	1.784
7	9.962	-2.962	8.773	0.881
28	22.057	5.943	35.319	1.601
3	1.346	1.654	2.736	2.032
6	2.691	3.308	10.943	4.665
1	5.962	-4.962	24.621	4.130
			Total	17.522

Degree of Freedom   =
Calculated X^2 value   = 17.522
Table X^2 value at 5% level   9.488

      Table 4.30 indicates that the calculated X^2 value is high than the table X^2 value at 5% level and hence the chi-square test reveals that the relationship between the work experience of employees and their attitude towards supervision is significant in Andipatti.

Null Hypothesis : Work experience of employees and
their attitude towards communication
is independent in Melur.

TABLE 4.31

Work Experience of Employees and their
Attitude towards Communication -
In Melur

X^2 - Test

O	E	O-E	$(O-E)^2$	$\dfrac{(O-E)^2}{E}$
4	1.931	2.069	4.281	2.217
8	6.534	1.466	2.149	0.329
3	6.535	-3.465	12.006	1.837
6	9.396	-3.396	11.533	1.227
31	31.802	-0.802	0.643	0.020
36	31.802	4.198	17.623	0.554
3	1.674	1.326	1.758	1.050
5	5.663	-0.663	0.440	0.078
5	5.663	-0.663	0.440	0.078
			Total	7.390

Degree of Freedom   = 4

Calculated X^2 value   = 7.390

Table X^2 value at 5% level 7.390

Table 4.31 indicates that the calculated x^2
value is less than the table value at 5% level and hence
the chi-square test indicates that the relationship between
the work experience of employee and their attitude towards
communication is insignificant in Melur.

Null Hypothesis : Work Experience of employees and
their attitude towards communi-
cation is independent in Andipatti.

TABLE 4.32

Work Experience of Employees and their Attitude
towards Communication - In
Andipatti
x^2 - Test

O	E	O-E	$(O-E)^2$	$\frac{(O-E)^2}{E}$
2	0.270	1.730	2.993	11.085
0	0.538	-0.538	0.289	0.538
0	1.192	-1.192	1.421	1.192
2	4.038	-2.038	4.153	1.029
6	8.077	-2.077	4.314	0.534
22	17.885	4.115	16.933	0.947
3	2.692	0.308	0.095	0.035
8	5.385	2.615	6.838	1.270
9	11.923	-2.923	8.544	0.717
			Total	17.347

Degree of Freedom   ▪   4

Calculated X^2 value   ▪   17.347

Table X^2 value at 5% level   9.488

        Table 4.32 indicates that the calculated X^2 value is high than the table X^2 value at 5% level and hence the chi-square test reveals that the relationship between the work experience of employees and their attitude towards communication is significant in Andipatti.

Null Hypothesis : Work experience of employees and their
attitude towards Organizational Climate
is independent in Melur

TABLE 4.33

Work Experience of Employees and their Attitude
towards Organizational Climate -
In Melur
x^2 - Test

O	E	O-E	$(O-E)^2$	$\frac{(O-E)^2}{E}$
3	1.545	1.455	2.117	1.370
8	10.168	-2.168	4.700	0.462
2	1.287	0.713	0.508	0.395
3	2.733	0.267	0.071	0.026
18	17.990	0.010	0.001	0.001
2	2.277	-0.277	0.077	0.034
3	2.495	0.505	0.255	0.102
15	16.426	-1.426	2.033	0.124
3	2.079	0.921	0.848	0.408
3	5.228	-2.228	4.964	0.949
38	34.416	3.584	12.845	0.373
3	4.356	-1.356	1.839	0.422
			Total	4.666

Degree of Freedom   =   6

Calculated x^2 value   =   4.666

Table x^2 value at 5% level   12.592

      Table 4.33 indicates that the calculated x^2 value is less than the table value at 5% level and hence the chi-square test reveals that the relationship between the work experience of employees and their attitude towards Organizational Climate is insignificant in Melur.

Null Hypothesis : Work experience of employees and their attitude towards Organizational Climate is independent in Andipatti.

TABLE 4.34

Work Experience of Employees and their
Attitude towards Organizational
Climate - In Andipatti
x^2 - Test

O	E	O-E	$(O-E)^2$	$\frac{(O-E)^2}{E}$
2	1.212	0.788	0.621	0.512
2	4.442	-2.442	5.963	1.342
3	1.346	1.654	2.736	2.033
4	2.423	1.577	2.486	1.026
5	8.885	-3.885	15.093	1.699
5	2.692	2.308	5.327	1.979
3	5.365	-2.365	5.593	1.042
26	19.673	6.327	40.031	2.035
2	5.962	-3.962	15.697	2.758
			Total	14.426

Degree of Freedom   = 4

Calculated x^2 value   = 14.426

Table x^2 value at 5% level 9.448

Table 4.34 indicates that the calculated x^2
value is high   than the table value at 5% level and hence
the chi-square test reveals that the relationship between
the work experience of employees and their attitude towards
Organizational Climate is significant in Andipatti.

From the above tests the following conclusions
have been drawn.

In Melur the work experience of the employee and
their attitude towards workers attitude, personnel policy,
performance reward relationship, supervision have significant relationship and with job characteristics, working
conditions, communication have insignificant relationship.

In Andipatti work experience of the employee and
their attitude towards workers attitude, working conditions,
personnel policy have insignificant relationship and job
characteristics, performance reward relationship, supervision
and communication have significant relationship.

Work experience of the employee and their attitude
towards Organizational Climate is insignificant in Melur
and significant in Andipatti. Hence the hypothesis - the
work experience of the employee influences their attitude

towards Organizational Climate is rejected in Melur and
accepted in Andipatti.

4.2.3   Income of the Employees Influences the Attitude
of Employee towards Organizational Climate :

TABLE 4.35

Income of the Employees and their
Average Mean Score

Income of the Employees	Melur		Andipatti	
	Number of Employees	Average Mean Score	Number of Employees	Average Mean Score
Upto 1000	4	147.343	9	136.675
1001 -2000	81	141.128	37	159.362
2001 and above	16	156.279	6	133.539
Total	101		52	

Table 4.35 shows that in Melur mill, employees
who belong to the higher income group consider the Organizational Climate to be good while the lower level income
groups are of the opinion that it is not good.

In Andipatti mill, employees who belong to the higher income group consider the Organizational Climate to be not good when compared to that of other income groups.

To test whether there is correlation between the income of the employees and their attitude towards Organizational Climate chi-square test has been applied.

Null Hypothesis : Income of employees and their attitude towards workers attitude is independent in Melur.

TABLE 4.36

Income of Employees and their Attitude
towards Workers Attitude - In
Melur

X^2 - Test

O	E	O-E	$(O-E)^2$	$\frac{(O-E)^2}{E}$
0	1.584	-1.584	2.509	1.584
35	32.079	2.921	8.532	0.266
5	6.337	-1.337	1.787	0.282
2	2.218	-0.218	0.048	0.021
44	44.911	-0.911	0.830	0.018
10	8.871	1.129	1.275	0.144
2	0.199	1.801	3.244	16.299
2	4.010	-2.010	4.040	1.007
1	0.891	0.109	0.012	0.013
			Total	19.634

Degree of Freedom = 4

Calculated X^2 value = 19.634

Table X^2 value at 5% level 9.488

Table 4.36 indicates that the calculated X^2 value
is higher than the table value at 5% level and hence the chi-
square test reveals that the relationship between the income
of employee and their attitude towards workers attitude is
significant in Melur.

Null Hypothesis : Income of employees and their attitude
towards workers attitude is independent
in Andipatti.

TABLE 4.37

Income of Employees and their Attitude towards
Workers Attitude-In Andipatti
X^2 - Test

O	E	O-E	$(O-E)^2$	$\dfrac{(O-E)^2}{E}$
2	2.423	-0.423	0.179	0.074
8	9.962	-1.962	3.849	0.386
4	1.615	2.385	5.688	3.522
3	5.538	-2.538	6.441	1.163
28	22.770	5.280	27.878	1.224
1	3.692	-2.692	7.247	1.963
4	1.038	2.962	7.247	6.982
1	4.270	-3.270	10.693	2.504
1	0.692	0.308	0.095	0.137
			Total	17.955

Degree of Freedom   =   4

Calculated x^2 value   =   17.955

Table x^2 value at 5% level   9.488

      Table 4.37 indicates that the calculated x^2 value is higher than the table value at 5% level and hence the chi-square test reveals that the relationship between the income of employees and their attitude towards workers attitude is significant in Andipatti.

Null Hypothesis : Income of employees and their attitude
towards job characteristics is indepen-
dent in Melur.

TABLE 4.38

Income of Employees and their Attitude towards
Job Characteristics - In Melur
x^2 - Test

O	E	O-E	$(O-E)^2$	$\frac{(O-E)^2}{E}$
2	1.028	0.972	0.945	0.919
12	20.881	-8.851	78.340	3.757
12	4.119	7.881	62.110	15.079
2	2.693	-0.693	0.480	0.178
63	54.537	8.463	71.622	1.313
3	10.772	-7.772	60.404	5.607
0	0.277	-0.277	0.077	0.277
6	5.614	0.386	0.149	0.026
1	1.109	-0.109	0.012	0.011
			Total	27.167

Degree of Freedom = 4

Calculated x^2 value = 27.167

Table x^2 value at 5% level 9.488

Table 4.38 indicates that the calculated x^2
value is higher than the table value at 5% level and hence
the chi-square test reveals that the relationship between
the income of employees and their attitude towards job
characteristics is significant in Melur.

Null Hypothesis : Income of employee and their attitude
towards job characteristics is indepen-
dent in Andipatti.

TABLE 4.39

Income of Employees and their Attitude towards
Job Characteristics - In
Andipatti
x^2 - Test

O	E	O-E	$(O-E)^2$	$\dfrac{(O-E)^2}{E}$
3	6.577	-3.577	12.795	1.945
33	27.038	5.962	35.545	1.315
2	4.385	-2.385	5.688	1.297
4	1.212	2.788	7.773	6.413
2	4.981	-2.981	8.886	1.784
1	0.807	0.193	0.037	0.046
2	1.212	0.788	0.621	0.512
2	4.981	-2.981	8.886	1.784
3	0.807	2.193	4.809	5.960
			Total	21.056

Degree of Freedom   =   4

Calculated x^2 value   =   21.056

Table x^2 value at 5% level   21.056

       Table 4.39 indicates that the calculated x^2 value is higher than the table value at 5% level and hence the chi-square test reveals that the relationship between the income of employees and their attitude towards job characteristics is significant in Andipatti.

Null Hypothesis : Income of employees and their attitude towards working conditions is independent in Melur.

TABLE 4.40

Income of Employees and their Attitude towards Working Conditions - In Melur

X^2 - Test

O	E	O-E	$(O-E)^2$	$\dfrac{(O-E)^2}{E}$
0	0.436	-0.436	0.190	0.436
8	8.822	-0.822	0.676	0.077
3	1.742	1.258	1.582	0.908
2	2.376	-0.376	0.141	0.660
54	48.119	5.881	34.586	0.719
4	9.505	-5.505	0.719	0.076
2	1.188	0.812	0.659	0.555
19	24.060	-5.060	25.604	1.064
9	4.752	4.248	18.045	3.797
			Total	7.692

Degree of Freedom   = 4

Calculated X^2 value   = 7.692

Table X^2 value at 5% level   9.448

Table 4.40 indicates that the calculated x^2 value is less than the table value at 5% level and hence the chi-square test reveals that the relationship between the income of the employees and their attitude towards working conditions is insignificant in Melur.

Null Hypothesis : Income of employees and their attitude towards working conditions is independent in Andipatti.

TABLE 4.41

Income of Employees and their Attitude towards Working Conditions - In Andipatti

x^2 Test

O	E	O-E	$(O-E)^2$	$\frac{(O-E)^2}{E}$
1	0.519	0.481	0.231	0.446
1	2.135	-1.135	1.288	0.603
1	0.346	0.654	0.428	1.236
4	4.327	-0.327	0.107	0.025
20	17.788	2.212	4.893	0.275
1	2.885	-1.885	3.553	1.232
4	4.154	-0.154	0.024	0.001
16	17.077	-1.077	1.160	0.008
4	2.769	1.231	1.515	0.547
			Total	4.433

Degree of Freedom   =   4

Calculated X^2 value   =   4.433

Table X^2 value at 5% level   9.488

        Table 4.41 indicates that the calculated X^2 value is less than the table value at 5% level and hence the chi-square test reveals that the relationship between the income of the employees and their attitude towards working conditions is insignificant in Andipatti.

Hull Hypothesis : Income of employees and their attitude
towards personnel policies is indepen-
dent in Melur.

TABLE 4.42

Income of Employees and their Attitude towards
Personnel Policies - In Melur
X^2 - Test

O	E	O-E	$(O-E)^2$	$\frac{(O-E)^2}{E}$
0	0.198	-0.198	0.039	0.198
1	4.010	-3.010	9.060	2.259
4	0.792	3.208	10.291	12.994
1	1.663	-0.663	0.440	0.264
33	33.683	-0.683	0.466	0.014
8	6.654	1.346	1.812	0.272
3	2.139	0.861	0.741	0.347
47	43.307	3.693	13.638	0.315
4	8.554	-4.554	20.739	2.424
			Total	19.087

Degree of Freedom = 4

Calculated X^2 value = 19.087

Table X^2 value at 5% level 9.488

Table 4.42 indicates that the calculated x^2 value is high than the table value at 5% level and hence the chi-square test reveals that the relationship between the income of employees and their attitude towards personnel policies is significant in Melur.

Null Hypothesis :   Income of employees and their attitude towards personnel policies is independent in Andipatti.

TABLE 4.43

Income of Employees and their Attitude towards
Personnel Policies - In Andipatti
x^2 - Test

O	E	O-E	$(O-E)^2$	$\left(\dfrac{O-E}{E}\right)^2$
4	3.115	0.885	0.783	0.251
9	12.808	-3.808	14.501	1.132
5	2.077	2.923	8.544	4.114
5	5.885	0.885	0.783	0.133
28	24.192	3.808	14.501	0.599
1	3.923	-2.923	8.544	2.178
			Total	8.407

Degree of Freedom   =   2

Calculated x^2 value   =   8.407

Table x^2 value at 5% level   5.991

       Table 4.43 indicates that the calculated x^2 value is higher than the table value at 5% level and hence the chi-square test reveals that the relationship between the income of the employees and their attitude towards personnel policies is insignificant in Andipatti.

Null Hypothesis : Income of the employees and their
attitude towards performance reward
relationship is independent in
Melur.

TABLE 4.44

Income of Employees and their Attitude towards
Performance Reward Relationship -
In Melur
X^2 - Test

0	E	O-E	$(O-E)^2$	$\dfrac{(O-E)^2}{E}$
0	0.119	-0.119	0.014	0.119
2	2.406	-0.406	0.165	0.068
1	0.475	0.525	0.270	0.580
0	1.228	-0.228	0.052	0.042
19	24.861	-5.861	34.351	1.382
12	4.911	7.099	50.396	10.262
4	2.653	1.347	1.814	0.583
60	53.733	6.267	39.275	0.731
2	10.614	-7.614	57.973	5.462
			Total	19.329

Degree of Freedom   = 4

Calculated X^2 value   = 19.329

Table X^2 value at 5% level 9.448

Table 4.44 indicates that the calculated x^2 value is higher than the table value at 5% level and hence the chi-square test reveals that the relationship between the income of employees and their attitude towards performance reward relationship is significant in Melur.

Null Hypothesis : Income of employees and their attitude towards performance reward relationship is independent in Andipatti

TABLE 4.45

Income of Employees and their Attitude towards
Performance Reward Relationship -
In Andipatti
x^2 - Test

O	E	O-E	$(O-E)^2$	$\dfrac{(O-E)^2}{E}$
0	0.173	-0.173	0.030	0.173
1	6.712	0.288	0.083	0.116
0	0.115	-0.115	0.013	0.115
7	2.596	4.404	19.395	7.471
3	10.673	-7.673	58.875	5.516
5	1.731	3.269	10.686	6.174
2	6.231	-4.231	17.901	2.873
33	25.615	7.385	54.538	2.129
1	4.154	-3.154	9.948	2.395
			Total	26.962

Degree of Freedom　　　　＝　4

Calculated x^2 value　　　＝　26.962

Table x^2 value at 5% level　9.448

      Table 4.45 indicates that the calculated x^2 value is higher than the table value at 5% level and hence the chi-square test reveals that the relationship between the income of employees and their attitude towards performance reward relationship is significant in Andipatti.

Null Hypothesis : Income of employees and their attitude

towards supervision is independent

in Melur

TABLE 4.46

Income of Employees and their Attitude towards
Supervision - In Melur
x^2 Test

O	E	O-E	$(O-E)^2$	$\frac{(O-E)^2}{E}$
1	0.634	0.366	0.134	0.211
11	12.832	-1.832	3.356	0.262
4	2.534	1.466	2.149	0.848
2	3.050	-1.050	1.103	0.361
65	61.752	4.248	18.046	0.292
10	12.198	-2.198	4.831	0.396
1	0.317	0.683	0.466	1.472
5	6.416	-1.416	2.005	0.313
2	1.267	0.733	0.537	0.424
			Total	4.579

Degree of Freedom = 4

Calculated x^2 value 4.579

Table x^2 value at 5% level 4.579

Table 4.46 indicates that the calculated x^2 value is less than the table value at 5% level and hence the chi-square test reveals that the relationship between the income of the employees and their attitude towards supervision is insignificant in Melur.

Null Hypothesis : Income of employees and their attitude towards supervision is independent in Andipatti.

TABLE 4.47

Income of Employees and their Attitude towards Supervision in Andipatti

x^2 Test

O	E	O-E	$(O-E)^2$	$\dfrac{(O-E)^2}{E}$
1	0.865	0.135	0.018	0.021
2	3.558	-1.558	2.427	0.682
2	0.577	1.423	2.025	3.509
4	6.404	-2.404	5.779	0.902
32	26.327	5.673	32.183	1.222
1	4.269	-3.269	10.686	2.503
4	1.731	2.269	5.148	2.974
3	7.115	-4.115	16.933	2.380
3	1.154	1.846	3.408	2.953
			Total	17.146

Degree of Freedom   = 4

Calculated x^2 value   = 17.146

Table x^2 value at 5% level 17.146

      Table 4.47 indicates that the calculated x^2 value is higher than the table value at 5% level and hence the chi-square test reveals that the relationship between the income of the employees and their attitude towards supervision is significant in Andipatti.

Null Hypothesis : Income of employees and their attitude
towards communication is independent
in Melur.

TABLE 4.48

Income of Employees and their Attitude towards
Communication - In Melur
x^2 - Test

O	E	O-E	$(O-E)^2$	$\frac{(O-E)^2}{E}$
0	0.594	-0.594	0.353	0.594
1	12.030	-11.030	121.661	10.113
14	2.376	11.624	135.117	56.867
3	2.891	0.109	0.012	0.001
68	58.545	9.455	89.397	1.527
2	11.564	-9.564	91.470	7.910
1	0.515	0.485	0.235	0.457
12	10.426	1.574	2.477	0.238
0	2.059	-2.059	4.239	2.059
			Total	79.766

Degree of Freedom = 4

Calculated x^2 value = 79.766

Table x^2 value at 5% level 9.488

Table 4.48 indicates that the calculated x^2 value is high than the table value at 5% level and hence the chi-square test reveals that the income of employees and their attitude towards communication is significant in Melur.

Null Hypothesis : Income of employees and their attitude towards communication is independent in Andipatti.

TABLE 4.49

Income of Employees and their Attitude towards Communication - In Andipatti

x^2 - Test

0	E	O-E	$(O-E)^2$	$\frac{(O-E)^2}{E}$
0	0.346	-0.346	0.120	0.346
0	1.423	-1.423	2.025	1.423
2	0.231	1.769	3.129	13.547
4	5.192	-1.192	1.421	0.274
22	21.346	0.654	0.428	0.020
4	3.462	0.538	0.289	0.084
5	3.462	1.538	2.365	6.683
15	14.231	0.769	0.591	0.042
0	2.307	-2.307	5.322	2.307
			Total	18.726

Degree of Freedom   = 4

Calculated X^2 value   = 18.726

Table X^2 value at 5% level   9.488

        Table 4.49 indicates that the calculated X^2 value is higher than the table value at 5% level and hence the chi-square test reveals that the relationship between the income of employees and their attitude towards communication is significant in Andipatti.

Null Hypothesis : Income of employees and their attitude
towards Organizational Climate is independent in Melur.

TABLE 4.50

Income of Employees and their Attitude towards
Organizational Climate - In Melur
x^2 - Test

O	E	O-E	$(O-E)^2$	$\frac{(O-E)^2}{E}$
1	0.475	0.525	0.276	0.581
1	3.129	-2.129	4.533	1.411
2	0.396	1.604	2.573	6.497
7	9.624	-2.624	6.885	0.715
71	63.356	7.644	58.431	0.922
3	8.020	-5.020	25.200	3.142
4	1.901	2.090	4.406	2.318
7	12.515	-5.515	30.415	2.430
5	1.584	3.416	11.669	7.367
			Total	25.383

Degree of Freedom   = 4

Calculated x^2 value   = 25.383

Table x^2 value at 5% level   9.488

Table 4.50 indicates that the calculated x^2 value is higher than the table value at 5% level and hence the chi-square test reveals that the relationship between the income of employees and their attitude towards Organizational Climate is significant in Melur.

Null Hypothesis : Income of employee and their attitude towards Organizational Climate is independent in Andipatti.

TABLE 4.51

Income of Employees and their Attitude towards Organizational Climate - In Andipatti

x^2 - Test

O	E	O-E	$(O-E)^2$	$\dfrac{(O-E)^2}{E}$
2	1.558	0.442	0.195	0.125
5	5.172	-0.172	0.507	0.089
2	1.731	0.269	0.072	0.042
4	6.404	-2.404	5.779	0.902
7	23.481	3.519	12.383	0.527
6	7.115	-1.115	1.243	0.175
3	1.037	1.963	3.853	3.716
1	3.808	-2.808	7.885	2.071
2	1.154	0.846	0.716	0.620
			Total	8.267

Degree of Freedom   =   4

Calculated x^2 value   =   8.267

Table x^2 value at 5% level   9.488

Table 4.51 indicates that the calculated x^2 value is less than the table value at 5% level and hence the chi-square test reveals that the relationship between the income of employee and their attitude towards Organizational Climate is insignificant in Andipatti.

From the above calculations, the following conclusions have been made.

The income of the employees and their attitude towards workers attitude, job characteristics, personnel policies, performance reward relationship, communication have significant relationship and towards working climate and supervision have insignificant relationship in Melur.

The income of the employees and their attitude towards workers attitude, job characteristics, performance reward relationship supervision and communication have significant relationship. The working conditions and personnel policies have insignificant relationship.

The relation between the income of the employees and their attitude towards Organizational Climate is significant in Melur and insignificant in Andipatti. Hence the hypothesis that the income of the employees influences their attitude towards Organizational Climate is accepted in Melur and rejected in Andipatti.

4.3 CONCLUSION

In this chapter, job factors influencing the attitude of the employees have been analysed by using chi-square test. To analyse the job factors influencing the Organizational Climate, the following hypotheses have been framed.

1) The Level of Management of the employee has influence over the Organizational Climate.

2) The Work experience of the employee has association with Organizational Climate.

3) The Income of the employee influences the attitude of the employees towards Organizational Climate.

In Melur, the analysis reveals that the Level of
Management and the Income of the employees have influence
over the attitude of the employees towards Organizational
Climate. The work experience of the employees has no
impact on their attitude towards Organizational Climate.

In Andipatti, the analysis reveals that the
level of management and the work experience have influence
over the attitude of the employees towards the Organizational
Climate. The income of the employees has no impact on
their attitude towards the Organizational Climate.

CHAPTER V

ORGANIZATIONAL CLIMATE - AN INFORMAL APPRAISAL

5.1   INTRODUCTION

Organizational Climate of one sector is different from another sector's Organizational Climate. It varies from one plant to another. In this chapter, existing Organizational Climate prevailing in the co-operative spinning mill sector in Madurai District has been high-lighted with the help of available records from the sele-cted units and observation made by the researcher during his visit to the selected units, interaction with employees and workers, and the views and opinions of the general public residing near the selected units are the other sources of information used to write this chapter.

5.2   PROFILE OF THE STUDY UNITS

Madurai District Co-operative Spinning Mill - Melur was started in the year 1965 November-1. 94% of the shares are held by the Government of TamilNadu. The rest of the shares are held by cotton growers and cotton purchasers.

Anna Co-operative Spinning Mill - Andipatti was started in the year 1984. 95% of the shares are held by

Government of TamilNadu and the rest of the shares are held by cotton growers and co-operative societies.

Madurai District Co-operative Spinning Mill has been situated between Melur and Thiruvadhavoor - 10 kms away from Madurai Corporation area and Anna Co-operative Spinning Mill is situated on Madurai-Theni Main Road between Andipatti and Theni.

Upto 17-07-1989 all the spinning mills in TamilNadu were managed by 8 members team headed by the District Collector which was appointed by Director of Handlooms and Textiles - Madras. As per the TamilNadu Government's special order the management committee was dissolved and a special officer has been appointed for every co-operative spinning mill unit to run the organization. He acted as Managing Director of the organization. Hiearchical structure of co-operative spinning mills clearly explains the function of co-operative spinning mills. (Vide Appendix-II)

The special officer has the power to take decisions regarding day to day operations of mill. He is the final decision making authority of the mill. He is answerable to the directorate of handlooms and textiles. Madras. The special officer of a co-operative spinning mill acts as a

link between mill' employees and directorate of handlooms
and textiles-Madras.

Regarding financial viability, Madurai District
Co-operative Spinning Mill is a sick mill. Sickness of
the unit has been decided on the basis of profitability
ratio, debt-equity ratio, current ratio, debtors velocity
and creditors velocity. On the basis of above calculation
the directorate of handlooms and textiles placed Madurai
District Co-operative Spinning Mill on the list of sick
units. Anna Co-operative Spinning Mill is a good working
Mill. It has the viability to meet its own debts and
expenses.*

5.3 EXISTING ORGANIZATIONAL CLIMATE IN MADURAI DISTRICT CO-OPERATIVE SPINNING MILL

In this study, Organizational Climate has been
analysed with the help of seven dimensions.

5.3.1 Workers Attitude

Workers attitude towards their belongingness to
the Organization has been neither low nor high. It is

---

* Data were not disclosed regarding Financial Viability,
  as it is related to the confidential nature of the
  department.

medium in this mill. Aged workers are in larger numbers
in this mill. Most of the aged workers have high degree
of belongingness to the organization. It is low in the
younger workers.

5.3.2 Job Characteristics

Nearly 85% of the workers are satisfied with
their job. Most of the workers stated that their educational qualification is very low. So, they have natural
involvement in the job which helps to earn money more than
they expected. Nearly 88% of the workers admitted that
they perform their function with full freedom.

5.3.3 Working Conditions

Nearly 70% of the workers are not satisfied with
their working conditions. More than 87% of the workers
complained about the poor ventilation facilities and toilet
facilities. The workload of the worker is different from
one department to another department. The workers in the
cone winding department complained that they suffer a lot
because of improper mixing. Due to the improper mixing
they are unable to finish the work assigned to them within
the stipulated time. So, they are punished with fine for
delay in the work.

5.3.4   Personnel Policies

Nearly 93% of the workers are not satisfied
with the personnel policies.   86% of the workers complained
about the unfavourable retirement benefits.   There is no
chance for promotion in this mill in the case of workers.
In the case of employees there is a limited scope for
promotion.   Selection is not made on the basis of ability
most of the employees and workers were recruited through
employment exchange and political influence..

5.3.5   Performance - Reward Relationship

Nearly 93% of the workers are not satisfied with
their salary.   Most of the respondents pointed out that
there is no encouragement to the worker who works hard and
has a better ability than others.   All the workers are
treated in same manner.   There is no special encouragement
to the skilled worker.

5.3.6   Supervision

Nearly 74% of the workers are satisfied with existing supervising procedures.   Nearly 76% of the workers

stated that the supervisors are interested in co-operating
with the workers. In the case of middle level management
there is high degree of intimacy with the top management.
Top management not at all pointed out single minus point
with their immediate supervisor.

5.3.7   Communication

In the co-operative spinning mills, there is very
meagre chance for communication gap. Top management and
middle management ruled out the chance for communication
gap. In lower level management, there is some informal
communication and friendly communication between workers
and top and middle management. .

5.4   EXISTING ORGANIZATIONAL CLIMATE IN ANNA
       CO-OPERATIVE SPINNING MILL

5.4.1   Workers Attitude

The belongingness to the organization is less
when compared to that of the Melur Co-operative Spinning
Mill. Most of the workers are young. They do not
show any respect to the management.. Most of the workers
like their working group. The middle level management

and top level management show higher degree of belongingness
towards the management. When compare to low level management.

5.4.2   Job Characteristics

Nearly 88% of the respondents in this mill are
satisfied with their job characteristics. They enjoy their
work. Though job characteristics get priority among the
given organizational dimensions there is lot of absentees
in this mill. Most of the workers belong to the surrounding area of the mill. They have some agricultural land.
The work on their land force the workers to take leave often
incurring loss of pay. This is not seen among the middle
level management and top management.

5.4.3   Working Conditions

Only around 7% of the respondents are satisfied
with the existing working conditions. In this mill also,
workers complained that the poor quality of cotton, results
in improper mixing. It affects the other department workers
badly. It generates dust and prevents the achievement of

the stipulated work loads etc.   The toilet facility and
ventilation facility are better than those in Melur Co-operative Spinning Mills.   The building structure is different
from that of the Melur unit.   So, it seems to be some what
better than that of the Melur unit.

5.4.4   Personnel Policies

Regarding personnel policies no workers are satisfied.
In this mill absenteesm is very high.   So, this mill mainly
is run with temporary workers.   It causes misunderstanding
between workers and management.   Understanding among the
work group is very high.   So, permanent workers very vigo-
rously attack the personnel policy of the unit.   This is
evident in both middle level and lower level management. Top
level management does not at all consider the personnel
policy important.   It follows the routine procedure of
recruting the worker through employment exchange.   But the
personnel policy of the mill is highly criticised by the
workers.

5.4.5   Performance - Reward Relationship

In all the levels of management there is dissatisfaction about their salary.   In the lower level, 83% of the

workers complained about the reward system existing in the
organization. In this mill also, encouragement to the
skilled worker is lacking.

5.4.6   Supervision

Regarding supervision there is controversial
opinion among workers. It differ from one worker to
another worker, In the middle level management, there
is some misunderstanding between the top management and
the middle management. This is clearly explicit from
the statements of the middle level management people.
The top management, is neither satisfied nor dissatisfied
with its immediate supervisors.

5.4.7   Communication

In this mill also communication is effectively
done. There is no communication gap in this mill. All
the matters pertaining to the mill are informed to all
the employees and workers immediately through circular,
notices on the board, informal information and inter communication cables. Communication facilities are highly
praised by all levels of management people in this mill.

5.5 CONCLUSION

The Organizational Climate of one unit is different
from the other unit's Organizational Climate. In   this
chapter the existing Organizational Climate in the Madurai
District Co-operative Spinning Mill and Anna Co-operative
Spinning Mill has been explained. The existing Organizational Climate is neither good nor bad in both the mills.
The working conditions in the Melur unit is poorer than
those in Andipatti unit. In Melur unit most of the workers
are highly experienced and aged. The aged workers feel
that they are unable to discharge their duties as fast as
they discharged while they were young. Younger workers
suggested that aged workers should be replaced by younger
workers with lesser wages. It will help to improve the
production of the mill. Regarding job characteristics
and communication, in all levels of management there is
high degree of satisfaction prevailing. The working condition, personnel policy, performance-Reward relationship
are not good. The supervision workers attitude are
moderate.

The Anna Co-operative Spinning Mill's personnel
policy is highly criticised by lower management. The top

management and middle management stated it as moderate.
The workers attitude, supervision, communication are
moderate. The performance-reward policy is not good in
all levels of management. The working condition is
better than that of the Melur unit.

This chapter has been drafted with the help of
informal talks with employees, workers of the respective
mills. People living around the mill, and the records
of selected units, are the other materials used as sources
to write this chapter. This helps to understand the
Organizational Climate dimensions. So, it will be very
easy to analyse the attitude of the workers in all levels
of management. The analysis of the attitude of different
levels of management has been drafted in the previous
chapter.

CHAPTER VI

SUMMARY AND CONCLUSION

6.1   INTRODUCTION

Organizational Climate is the human environment
within which an organization's employees do their work.
Organizational Climate serves as the guideline for deal-
ing with people, and has a major influence on motivation
and productivity of individuals as well as total work
group.   Climate, in a natural sense, is referred to as
the average course or conditions of the weather at a place
over a period of years as exhibited by temperature, wind
velocity, and precipitation.   However, it is quite
difficult to define Organizational Climate incorporating
the characteristics of natural climate.   Just as the
presence of air is feet in human survival, the climate is
evidenced by the survival of an organization.   Hence,
it is necessary to maintain a good, relationship among the
three constituents man, machine and management.   It is
clear from the foregoing chapters that an employee's
individual personality and his way of perceiving the work
situation are important determinants of his performance.

Each worker in an organization has to do his best
for the development of himself and his organization to which

he belongs. The way to ensure this is to create such a
climate in an organization, where the workers have to
satisfy their social and psychological needs besides their
economic needs. Good climate reduces absentism, strikes
and labour turnover in an organization.

Textile industry is one of the traditional industry
in India. In TamilNadu, Madurai district has heavy concentration of textile units. Just like other textile units
in other parts of the country in Madurai also textile units
are suffering a lot both from the view point of employers
and employees. How far the Organizational Climate in
textile units is conducive for maintaining a good relationship between the employers and employees? In the present
study an attempt has been made to study the existing
organizational climate and the attitude of employees towards
Organizational Climate in co-operative spinning mills in
Madurai district. To study the Organizational Climate the
following dimensions have been analysed (i) workers attitude,
(ii) Job characteristics (iii) Working conditions (iv)
personnel policies (v) performance reward relationship
(vi) supervision (vii) communication.

6.2   EXISTING ORGANIZATIONAL CLIMATE IN CO-OPERATIVE
       SPINNING MILLS

The existing Organizational Climate of the selected
units have been decided on the basis of observation, conver-
sation with various level of management people, and secondary
sources available from the selected units.   The existing
Organizational Climate has been analysed only from the view
point of the employees.   It helps to analyse the workers'
attitude towards Organizational Climate and to identify the
factors responsible for existing Organizational Climate.

More or less the same kind of Organizational Climate
is prevailing in Melur unit (Sick Mill) and Andipatti unit
(Good working mill).   The Organizational Climate of co-operative spinning mills is in no way related to productivity.
The same kind of procedures, and production methods have been
adopted in both the mills.   Melur unit has the experience
of nearly 27 years but Andipatti mill has only 7 years
experience but both the mills have the same level of production and the same kind of techniques are being adopted.
The Organizational Climate can be determined by analysing
the dimensions already mentioned.

In General, the Organizational Climate is better
in Andipatti than in Melur unit.   The workers attitude
helps to identify their belongingness to management.
Melur unit workers have more belongingness than Andipatti
unit workers.   Regarding job characteristics more or less
the same kind of attitude is shown in both the mills.
Most of them have favourable attitude towards their job.
Regarding working conditions in both the units, workers
showed their displeasure.   In Andipatti mill only 7%
of the workers showed favourable attitude towards working
conditions.   Regarding personnel policies very few have
favourable attitude in both the mills.   In Melur, complaints about the poor retirement benefit are numerous. In
Andipatti mill the workers show their displeasure regarding temporary workers position.

Regarding performance reward relationship a very
high degree of negative attitude is prevailing among all
levels of management.   More or less all the employees
feel that they do not get any encouragement from the top
management and express their displeasure regarding salary
and bonus.   Regarding supervision in Melur mill complaints
are very few in top and middle level management but in
lower level management 25% of the employees are not at all

satisfied with their supervisors. Regarding communication
more or less-in all levels of management, people are favour-
ably disposed.

6.3   WORKERS ATTITUDE TOWARDS ORGANIZATIONAL CLIMATE

The employees attitude towards Organizational
Climate is "moderate" in both Melur unit and Andipatti
unit.   78.22% of employees consider the climate as
'Moderate' in Melur. 63.46% of employees regard the
Organizational Climate as 'Moderate' in Andipatti unit.
To analyse the attitude of employees towards Organizational
Climate Likert Scale has been used.   In seven dimensions
seven statements have been given and the respondents were
asked to state whether they strongly agree (5), Agree(4)
or have no opinion (3) Disagree (2) or strongly disagree(1)
to the statements.   Their response has been classified
into three groups viz., High level attitude, medium level
attitude and low level attitude by using mean, standard
deviation, mean deviation of each respondents score. To
verify the factors influencing the Organizational Climate
the following hypotheses have been framed.

i) The age of the employees influences their attitude towards Organizational Climate.

ii) The education of the employees influences their attitude towards Organizational Climate.

iii) The social group of the employees influences their attitude towards Organizational Climate.

iv) The level of management of the employees influences their attitude towards Organizational Climate.

v) The work experience of the employees influences their attitude towards Organizational Climate.

vi) The income of the employees influences their attitude towards Organizational Climate.

The hypotheses have been tested by using chi-square test. In Melur, the analysis reveals that age, education, level of management, income, social group have influence over employees attitude towards Organizational Climate. Work experience of the employees has no impact on their attitude towards Organizational Climate.

In Andipatti, the analysis reveals that age,
level of management, work experience have influence over
the attitude of employees towards Organizational Climate.
Education, Income and social group of the employee does
not influence their attitude towards Organizational Climate.

6.4 FINDINGS

The Organizational Climate of Co-operative
spinning mills in Madurai district is Moderate. This
is expressed by employees when the data had been collected.
In both the mills job characteristics have been described
to be good. To analyse the involvement in job, the
respondents were asked to rank the following. A) Job
B) Boss C) Work Group D) Organization E) Environment.
In both the mills job was ranked first by most of the
employees. 72% of employees ranked it best among the
above said five factors in Melur and 69% in Andipatti.
Aged employees with more work experience are reluctant to
go for other jobs even if they get a chance in other
organizations. Only 34% of the employee were prepared
to go out and accept jobs with better prospects 2% of the
employees wish to go for other jobs though the jobs have
benefits same as they are enjoying now in other organizations

when the employees were asked whether they would work for
the overall development of the mill if they are offer   a
chance except 2 employee the others were readily to accept
the offer.   Every one has showed his readiness to work
for the over all development of the mill.

Regarding working conditions, in both the mills
employees complained about poor canteen facilities and
cleanliness in the mill.   The tea provided by the management during working hours was said to be not good.   Regarding personnel policies and performance reward relationship
both the mill workers expressed their dissatisfaction.
Aged people in Melur unit expect their legal heirs to be
given jobs when they retire or their pension to be settled.
They feel that they will become helpless when they retire.
Regarding supervision, the employees feel that they have
moderate relationship with their superiors in both the
mills.   In both the mills the lower level employees criticise
the attitude of labour welfare officer and other top management officials.   In middle management the employees feel
that they find it difficult to maintain good relationship
with top level management, and workers.   They strongly feel
that the people in other management levels do not understand
their problems.   Communication system is regarded to be
good by all levels of management people in both the mills.

6.5   SUGGESTIONS

From the above study the following suggestions
have been made.

i)   The overall climate of the organization
should be improved by paying special attention to the
dimensions personnel policies, performance reward
relationship and working conditions.

ii)   A significant improvement in the overall
performance of the workers could be brought about by
motivating them properly through workers education.

iii)   Interrelationship between different levels
of management can improved by setting up of grievance
cell in every unit.

iv)   Frequent transfer of top official should
be avoided.

v)   To remove caste feelings among mill workers
in Melur unit, proper steps should be taken by the management through effective workers.   Education programmes
which will infuse in them a feeling of unity.

vi)   Barring ESI, no other facilities are provided
by the directorate of handlooms and textiles, Madras. So,
steps should be taken to provide, housing patta in Melur
mill and Andipatti mill to make the workers happy.

6.6   CONCLUSION

This dissertation is a modest attempt to measure
the Organizational Climate of co-operative spinning mills
in Madurai district.   The Organizational Climate of co-
operative spinning mills in Madurai district has been
analysed with the co-operation of workers of co-operative
spinning mills in Melur (sick unit) and Andipatti (good
working mill).   It is found out that the Organizational
Climate of the co-operative spinning mills in Madurai
district is perceived to be "Moderate" by employees of
all levels of management.   Productivity is not at all
related with Organizational Climate in co-operative spinning mills.   The textile industry plays a pivotal role
in the development of economy.   Good Organizational Climate
of an industry helps the industry to progress.   Hence it
is important to study the Organizational Climate of co-operative spinning mills.

CPSIA information can be obtained
at www.ICGtesting.com
Printed in the USA
BVHW081159190223
658756BV00002B/403

9 784681 966602